I0827456

Wm. G. Justice
DMin, DPhil, DLitt

What If Jesus Remained In the Tomb?

World Changes Brought About By Christianity

GlobalEdAdvance Press
37321-7635

What If Jesus Remained in the Tomb?

Library of Congress Control Number: 2008943754

Justice, William G.,1930 -
What If Jesus Remained in the Tomb?
ISBN 978-1-935434-02-3

Subject Codes and Description
1: REL Religion: Christianity-History-General;
2: REL Religion: Christian Theology – History;
3: REL Religion: Christian Life - General

Printed in the United States of America

Published by
GlobalEdAdvance Press
37321-7635 USA

Other Books by Author

Don't Sit on the Bed
(A Handbook for Visiting the Sick)

Guilt and Forgiveness
How God Can Help You Feel Good About Yourself

Guilt, the Source and the Solution
(Defense Systems to Avoid Feeling Guilty)

When Death Comes
(A Handbook for Pastors and Laypersons
Who Minister to the Bereaved)

When Your Patient Dies
(A Handbook for Physicians and Nurses
Who Minister to Families at the Time of a Patient's Death)

Jesus' Silent Years
Exploring Facts the Gospels Do Not Tell Us

God in the Hands of Angry Sinners

Jesus the Maverick King

The Nature of God as Revealed in Jesus

Training Guide for Visiting the Sick
More Than a Social Call

When God Seems Silent

Damned if We Are Not Forgiven
Understanding Guilt and People Who Are Their Own Worst Enemies

Contents

Chapter 3

Chapter 4

To

Harley Dixon

Retired hospital chaplain

and

My friend for almost half a century

Who has changed his world one person at a time

Introduction

What if Jesus remained in the tomb? If He had not resurrected from the dead, the world in which you and I live would be a very different place. A few years ago, during lunch, a friend looked across the table and soberly announced, "Bill, Christianity just isn't working." Although I had to admit that he was more accurate than I could comfortably admit, I also began to look at the great accomplishments brought about by Christianity's influence upon the world and especially upon the societies into which Christianity has been integrated. I knew that my life had been transformed by the power of God in Christ, and I had seen the lives of others transformed. But what greater spheres of life had been transformed? In many ways, Christianity has dramatically redirected the course of world history by initiating change in whole societies.

The Gospel of Christ was intended to promote change in the people to whom Jesus ministered. He expected those who changed to further influence change in the societies of Jerusalem and Judea, and on into Samaria and Galilee and ultimately into the whole world. He envisioned a time in which the whole world would encompass the Kingdom of God: the realm in which the hearts of all humankind would submit to the rule of God as King. Change would begin in individuals and spread to influence whole societies. The purpose of this publication is to make a brief historical overview of some of the most significant contributions that Christianity has made to the world—contributions that seem generally unrecognized by men and women of the modern day. Sociology is the systematic study of the development, structure, interaction, and collective behavior of organized groups (societies) of human beings. This is a historical-sociological study of representative high points in history in which changes in societies have been brought about by the influence of Christianity with examples of societies' unfortunate influences on Christianity at various periods in history. Perhaps the reader will be challenged to help change the current society by contributing to the change one person at a time.

Although we will review some of the high points in the history of the positive influence of the Christian religion on various societies, we also will review some of the low points in history in which society has negatively influenced Christianity. All change is not progress. Too often, when Christianity has been unable to effectively integrate a society the change has been regressive.

This study acknowledges the bias that Jesus, the Christ (the Messiah) came to change the world into a better habitat for humanity, and He intended for His followers to pursue that task until the end of the age in which humankind lives on earth.

It is my hope, and my prayer that the reader will be challenged to examine and implement opportunities to participate in the process of changing the world into a better place. With few exceptions, world changers have been common, ordinary people who have shared a common magnificent obsession–ordinary people who have made a difference in the lives of those around them. People, societies, and the world are changed one person at a time. Who can guess what triumphs lay ahead?

David Ward, a doctoral candidate at Oxford Graduate School who served as my research assistant and Dr. Eunice Reynolds, my friend, who readied the original text syllabus for use by students at Oxford Graduate School are both due special words of gratitude for their pertinent observations. Dave has an unusual ability to find resources. He seems to be able to enter a library, sniff the air, and go straight to books on subjects about which he wants information. Dr. Reynolds has retired as Dean of Oxford Graduate School after having helped numerous doctoral candidates refine their dissertations. Dr. Reynolds, by applying her unusual skills and creative thoughts, has helped refine this manuscript as did my dear friend, Barbara Barbee.

Thanks, Dave. Thanks, Eunice. Thanks Barbara. Thanks for your help, but since I have not always followed advice, I alone must accept responsibility for the content of the pages ahead.

Chapter 1

Foundations of Jesus' Troubled Society

The age into which Jesus (the Christ, the Messiah, the King) was born, like all other ages before and since His time, was shaped by its predecessors. Even a line of falling dominos a mile long ultimately impacts the last domino standing.

Foundations Built by Alexander the Great

Roughly 300 years before Jesus' birth, Alexander the Great, a Greek warrior prince had conquered virtually all lands between the Atlantic Ocean and Northwest India. Even after three centuries, Jesus' Palestine struggled under the daily influence of Alexander's successors who continued to foster Alexander's ideals.

With the passing of years, as a domino knocks down a domino that knocks down a domino, Palestine was "knocked down" by the Assyrians under the rule of Antiochus IV Epiphanies. This led to some of the bloodiest and cruelest days in

Jewish history as Antiochus forced every effort to eradicate Judaism from the face of the earth. Despite the eventual overthrow of the Assyrians, each new ruler became another oppressor. The Jews found themselves only exchanging one oppressor for another. Bloody uprisings continued. As one domino knocks down another, in a chain reaction, each event in history initiates another event.

Weakened by a century of repeated rebellions, the Romans saw Palestine as a weak plum too tempting to leave unplucked. In 63 BC, Roman general Pompey, killing 12,000 Jews took the city of Jerusalem. The Jews were not a meek people. By the time Herod the Great arrived on the scene, in 37 BC, no fewer than 150,000 Jews had died in revolutionary uprisings against the Romans. The Jews of Palestine became so troublesome that at one period, the Romans occupied twenty-two fortresses throughout the land.

When Jesus was born, Caesar Augustus, commonly known as "the Savior" and "Prince of Peace" ruled the Roman Empire. After having had a crown of gold placed on his head by Caesar Augustus, Herod the Great was given rule over Palestine with the title, "King of the Jews." The High Priest of the great Temple in Jerusalem, after having paid Caesar Augustus for his office, ruled all religious and many civil affairs among the Jews. Since his authority sometimes conflicted with the authority of Herod, no one was surprised that bad blood flowed between the two men. Both were easy to hate. However, the general population had far greater issues to concern them.

Alexander had had a dream. He wanted to unify the world—to create a world unified by Greek language, Greek culture, the Greek religions and all else that made Greeks, Greeks. Quickly following Alexander's untimely death, the generals whom Alexander had left behind to rule in his name assumed the position as regional monarchs. Those rulers continued Alexander's dream. All people in all lands were expected to adopt all facets of the Greek culture.

Rome became busy at building up a mighty fighting machine—an army of 300,000 well-trained, well-disciplined men with a "ready reserve" of an additional 300,000 able fighting men. These could be called to "active duty" with brief warning. With the passing of time, the mighty Roman armies conquered all of the lands that Alexander had conquered earlier.

Since the Romans were enamored by virtually everything related to the Greeks (the Helens), they fully supported all efforts to forcibly change the people of all lands they ruled. Historians commonly refer to this effort as the period of "Hellenization" of all people ruled by the Romans to adapt to all facets of the Greek society. They wanted all peoples to become fully Hellenized—to fully accept every aspect of the Greco-Roman culture as their own.

Many Jews were yielding to the religious and social pressures. Since Roman sporting events were conducted in the nude, young Jewish men were experiencing ridicule by their Roman counterparts for having been circumcised. They taunted the Jewish boys saying that Roman gods would never make such a demand on their followers. Many of these young Jewish men were even undergoing surgery to hide the evidence of their having been circumcised. (We are left to wonder how this was accomplished.) To the devout Jew, this "un-circumcision" signified the departure from the Jewish faith by disobedience to instructions from YHWH (Yahweh/Jehovah) their God. The pagan religions were taking a heavy toll on the Jewish society. (Little did those young men realize that Cybele, the "Mother of the Gods," required men to ritually castrate themselves.)

Yet other factors were enticing the Jews to turn from the worship of Yahweh, the God of Father Abraham and Moses. Every city of significance had its own amphitheater to which people flocked by the thousands to hear the preaching of the newest and the oldest Greek and Roman philosophical/ religious teachings. The more bizarre teachings drew the largest crowds. The Jewish society with its religion was slowly eroding as one by one the people were rejecting the God of their fathers to worship the gods of the Greeks and Romans. That which the Greeks and Romans had not been able to accomplish with the sword was being accomplished by wandering, orators–preachers. Of course this process was hastened by the social impact of Romans who were infiltrating the society with their Greco-Roman religion's philosophies.

If the religion does not change the society, the society will change the religion.

Old Foundations Built by Yahweh Worshipers

Within Judaism, no division existed between the religion, government, and the society. They were inseparably interwoven–inseparably integrated into the lives of the people. Throughout their history of more than two thousand years, many had strayed from the faith of their fathers. But no matter how far the majority wandered from the path commanded by their God, a remnant of the people remained faithful. They were guided by the Law of Moses, centering on the Ten Commandments and the Torah—the sacred writings Christians know as the Biblical books of Genesis, Exodus, Leviticus, Numbers, and Deuteronomy.

Some Resisted the Religious-Social Changes

When the Roman society began to strongly influence the religion-society of the Jews, one group became totally disgusted with their own people. Fearing total contamination of the faith of their people, they came out from among the major population centers of their people and established separate communities. These, we know as the Essenes who thrived in remote communities. The best known of those communities was at Qumran—the place that for centuries remained the hiding place for the documents we now call the "Dead Sea Scrolls."

Others resisted the change with a rebellious spirit. A major rebellion was destined to spark only four miles from Jesus' boyhood home in Nazareth. Of course, it too was the fruit of seeds planted in earlier years.

Warring against Pompey in 48-47 BC, Julius Caesar found a warrior named Antipater to be an able leader. Shortly thereafter, as a reward for his loyal service, Julius Caesar gave Antipater rule over much of Palestine with the title of Procurator. Antipater, in turn, made Herod his twenty-six year old son Governor of Galilee. In the growing city of Sepphoris, roughly four miles from the little community of Nazareth, Herod built his first of what would become six castle-fortresses. [He would later build one at Jericho, one on the coast at Caesarea Maritima, another, Marchaerys, the "Black Fortress" in Perea, nine miles east of the Dead Sea, another (the Herodium) between Bethlehem and Jerusalem, and in honor of his friend, Mark Anthony, he built the Antonia adjacent to the Temple in Jerusalem.] Having fled to Messada before he became king, Herod felt that that fortress needed additional security and included it in his massive building program.

Although Herod had begun his career as a ruler governing only the region of Galilee, he soon caught the attention of Rome when he effectively and quickly put down an insurrection in his territory. When his father had died, Rome declared Herod "King of the Jews." By the time Herod died, the land was seething with rage against the Romans. Heavy taxes burdened the people. Caesar Augustus was haled as a savior-god who would reign for a thousand years as the Prince of Peace. As such, he was to be worshipped.

The society represented by the occupying Roman forces was causing too much change for the Jews. In Herod's will, his son, Archelaus was given rule over Judea and Samaria. Herod Antipas was awarded Galilee. However, a new king was coming, not to rule Judea, Samaria, and Galilee, but to rule the world.

The World Expected a Universal Ruler to Arise Out of Judea

For centuries before "the days of Herod, the King," sages had predicted the coming of a great prophet—a world-ruling King who would be born in the land of Judea. Prophets had come before Him and prophets have come since Him, but none other has been expected for centuries and none other has been foretold by renowned seers of virtually all societies across the globe from the Italian Peninsula to China.

The Romans Were Foretelling His Coming

During the latter half of the first century BC, the Romans ruled virtually every acre from Britain to the Indus River, of India, and much of the North African continent. With local kings ruling with an iron fist under the authority of Caesar Augustus and the Roman Senate, Herod the Great sustained an unsteady semblance of the *Pax Romana:* the

Roman Peace. Augustus had dedicated himself so strongly to the preservation of peace, that his people had dubbed him "the Prince of Peace." However, in Herod's kingdom, the land that provided a route that connected Europe, Asia, and Africa, the oppressed Jews allowed little peace for their rulers. Every Jew was certain that, "The King is coming soon to deliver us. The Lord (God) delivered our forefathers from bondage in Egypt and when Messiah (God's anointed, Christ/King) comes, He will deliver us from the Roman rule." Yet, even while Romans ruled, some prominent Roman writers shared the spirit of anticipation that awaited the rise of a great king from out of Judea.

Speaking of his own people, the Romans, Tacitus wrote, "People are generally persuaded in the faith of the ancient prophesies, that the East was to prevail, and that from Judea was to come the Master and Ruler of the world." Suetonius, in his account of the life of Vespasian said, "It was an old and constant belief throughout the East, that by indubitably certain prophecies, the Jews were to attain the highest power. . . .Out of Judah would come 'mastery over the world."[1]

Greeks Were Foretelling His Coming

In Greece, during their people's troubled times Aeschylus wrote, "Look not for any end, moreover, to this curse until God appears, to accept upon His Head the pangs of thy own sins

---

1 Ann Wroe, *Pontius Pilate*, (New York: Random House, 1999), p. 137

vicarious." Cicero wrote about a "King whom we must recognize to be saved." The Fourth Eclogue of Virgil, after writing of the same belief, spoke of "a chaste woman, smiling on her infant boy, with whom the iron-age would pass away." He also spoke of a forthcoming golden child "filled with the life of the gods" who would bring in a kingdom of love, where the sins of humankind would fade away.[2]

Jews Were Foretelling His Coming

Of course, in the land of Palestine, for more than 700 years, the prophets of Jehovah had been foretelling the coming of a king greater than King David, who had been the king of the Hebrew Kingdom's "Golden Age." Isaiah had foretold, *"For unto us a child is born, unto us a son is given; and the government shall be upon his shoulder; and his name shall be called Wonderful, Counselor, The mighty God, The everlasting Father, The Prince of Peace."*[3] The Pharisees sited more than 450 references to the Messiah within the Torah (the first five books of the Old Testament), and more than 240 additional references in the writings of the Prophets. These were supported by more than 550 references to the Messiah in the most ancient Rabbinic writings. Every Jew knew that God was going to send His "anointed one," a king–the Messiah.

---

2 *Ibid*, p. 137.

3 Isaiah 9:6.

Persians Were Foretelling His Coming

Hundreds of miles farther east, from the mountains of Moab, in the edge of Persia, a prophet had written, “A star shall rise out of Jacob and a scepter shall spring up from Israel.” We can reasonably suspect that this prophesy was responsible for the “wise men”/magi having made their journey into Judea after they spotted the new “star” in their western sky.

Chinese Were Foretelling His Coming

Many hundreds of miles still farther east, sages in China, anticipated a great Wise Man who would arise from their west: “In the 24th year of Tchao-Wang of the dynasty of the Tcheou, on the 8th day of the 4th moon, a light appeared in the Southwest which illuminated the king’s palace. The monarch, struck by its splendor, interrogated the sages. They showed him books in which this prodigy signified the appearance of the great Saint of the West whose religion was to be introduced into this country.”

In the course of world history, many men have been viewed as gods, but at no time in history has the coming of a god been foretold for hundreds of years, by peoples from throughout the known inhabited world. The more we study the life of this king, the more we see that God’s way of doing things is different—far higher than ours.

The King was coming, but who would have expected Him to arrive as a baby born a to teen-aged Jewish peasant girl? He would even enter the world as a maverick. Tradition held that a king was the offspring of a royal family. Jesus would enter the world differently than other people do—the child of a virgin.

Chapter 2

Jesus Arrived in an Upside Down World

The Whole World Seemed Hostile

Probably in AD 6, a decree went out from Caesar Augustus that required a census to be taken for the purpose of gathering information to help the Roman government to estimate the amount of tax they could expect from across the Empire. Of course, such a census would also help them to boast of the number of people under their rule. Rome, no longer considering Palestine an "occupied land" officially annexed it as a part of the Empire. For many Jews, the decree for the census was the "last straw." Nothing could have stamped "Roman Rule" on the Jews more than that command.

The Jews were required to return to the city in which their ancestor's records were maintained for the filing of the appropriate documents. (Virtually every Jew had been taught to read and write.) This occasion pulled thousands of angry, militant Jews into clusters across the land. Since a rebellion was on the mind of virtually every person, the results were almost predictable. All they needed for a revolutionary explosion was a strong personality to take the lead and a fight for freedom would be underway.

One arose. Judas, the son of Ezekias with a band of angry Galileans came swinging a bloody sword and screaming the battle cry, “None but The Lord is Israel’s master.” This band of angry Galileans stormed the palace-fortress at Sepphoris and was soon inside the armory. They quickly took all of the swords, shields, spears, slings, slinger balls, bows and arrows, and other weapons and handed them out to any able-bodied man who would join the fight. They had declared war on the forces of Rome. The fighting quickly spread throughout Palestine. Josephus, the Jewish historian, described the fighting that resulted from the rebellion as “a great slaughter.”

Roman Legionnaires from Syria rushed down to support the Roman troops who had occupied the land since 63 BC. From the village of Nazareth, perched on a hillside overlooking Sepphoris less than four miles away, we can reasonably assume that the frightened residents of Nazareth watched the flames and smoke rise from the city of Sepphoris as it burned during the final struggle between the Romans and the valiant Galileans. When the fighting ceased, the Romans crucified 2000 men and took thousands more into slavery. Crucifixion was more than a way of punishing rebels against the state. It was a way of saying,

"This is what we do to enemies of the Empire. Don't let this happen to you!"

Troubled were the times when a Galilean builder named Joseph and his pregnant young wife, Mary, trudged their way from Nazareth in Galilee to Bethlehem via the twenty foot wide, paved concrete Roman highway. As a descendant of the great king David, Joseph and his wife had to go to Bethlehem to register for the required Roman census. While in Bethlehem, Mary gave birth to a son whom they named Jesus. After a period (perhaps about two years) the family moved to Egypt where they are believed to have lived in a large Jewish community—descendants of the remnant of Jews who had remained behind when Moses and a large number of Jews fled Egypt approximately 1400 years earlier. After a few years in Egypt, Joseph, Mary, and their young son, Jesus, returned to Palestine and settled at the hillside village of Nazareth. There, the boy seems to have lived the normal life of a Jewish boy of his era, learning the builder's craft and attending the local school for the next ten years as required by law.[4]

Jesus Launched His Ministry in Galilee

Whatever the impact of the Roman efforts to influence the religion of the Jews of the rest of the region, the New Testament gives no indication of their influence on the people of the little town

---

4 Wm. G. Justice, *Jesus' Silent Years: Exploring Facts the Gospels Do Not Tell Us*, (Bloomington, IN: 1st Books, 2004) pp. 94-100.

of Nazareth. However, the ministry of one of Nazareth's citizens was destined to change much of the society in which He lived and much of the world for the next 2000 years and beyond.

That citizen was Jesus, whom many came to know as the Messiah—the Christ—the King of the Kingdom of God. Brandishing no sword, this revolutionist conquered the hearts of men and women gaining followers with His effective use of the spoken word and His attitude toward God and people. These were supported by His treatment of the people he encountered—His unceasing demonstration of the form of love that habitually works in the best interests of others. He inspired trust–faith in those who knew Him best.

Jesus the Maverick

In modern language we have to view this king as a maverick. He was different. Failing to follow the tradition of other kings, He invited, but forced no one to accept Him as their Lord—as their ruler. He refused to follow the thinking of the crowd. He refused to follow the traditions of His own people. He refused to act as others expected Him to act. He was a maverick.

Lest the reader clearly understands the meaning of the word "maverick" one might consider the term inappropriate or even disrespectful. Therefore, let us briefly step aside from the path of our thought and look at the word, maverick.

In the mid 1800's, a frontiersman named Maverick refused to brand his calves. Of course, this made his calves stand out as different than others. He broke tradition. He broke from the expectations of other cattle growers. If someone spoke of his unbranded calf, he might say, "There's a Maverick calf". Soon, one simply pointed to an unbranded calf and said, "There's a Maverick," leaving off the obvious fact that it was a calf. The saying became so popular that any thing or any person that stood out as breaking custom, expectations, teachings, or tradition was called a maverick. The maverick had no peers.

With all due respect for my Lord, Jesus of Nazareth fits the definition of a maverick. He refused to live by the expectations, the customs, the teachings, or traditions of his countrymen. He broke with their beliefs, their practices, their world-view, and their understanding of the nature of God. Not only was He a maverick, he was also a king.[5]

Much of what He said was contrary to their way of thinking, teaching, and behaving. Almost every word Jesus spoke and everything Jesus did seemed to be in reverse of the way everyone in His culture was accustomed to thinking and doing. Everyone viewed Him as an independent individual who refused to go along with the traditions and practices of the people around Him—a maverick. He insisted that He was dependent on the Father in Heaven. He even failed to do things the way we would have expected Him to do them. Because His words and behaviors were so far off the beaten path

5 Wm. G. Justice, *Jesus the Maverick King*, (Bloomington, In. Author-House, 2004). p. viii).

of our own way of life, people of the modern era are also inclined to reject Him as God's anointed King of the Kingdom of Heaven here on earth.

His perspective on that which is best for people was quite different from that of most who heard him speak. Although thousands came out into the countryside from the surrounding cities, towns, and villages to hear Him, few followed for more than a short time. The masses quickly concluded that neither His words nor His actions met their expectations for God's Anointed One–God's Savior King—the Messiah.

Jesus? A King? He was a peasant—a common man who labored with his hands—a builder and the son of a builder. Some even whispered the rumor that even though Jesus may have been Joseph's son, Mary had conceived Him before she married. (Later discreditors claimed that he was the son of a Roman soldier.) The fickle masses had trouble believing that He was even a prophet. Virtually, everything he said and did was backward. Even His identity was backward. A peasant king? Peasants do not become kings. Ridiculous!

Almost everything He said ran counter to everything the people around Him believed. "You believe we should love our enemies? Everyone knows we are supposed to hate our enemies. You want us to forgive? Forget it! We will retaliate against anyone who harms us or ours, in keeping with the teachings of our forefathers for at least 2000 years."

Everyone was aware that the Scribes, the Pharisees, and the Sadducees knew how righteous people should behave. These prestigious men were the "elders." They knew the Scriptures. They knew the traditions of their forefathers, and they ably taught them to the people. This Jesus person repeatedly spoke and behaved in violation of their traditions. He was truly the Non-Traditional Man of His era, refusing to fit the mold that others wanted to create for Him.

Within the framework of their culture, much that Jesus said and did made no sense. Nor does He make sense to much of our world today. Most of what He taught ran counter to the beliefs of His people. Much of what He taught about God ran counter to what they believed about God. It still does. Everyone has a perception of the personality of God. (Even those who deny that God exists, have a perception of the god in which they do not believe.) Few choose to accept the perception of the Father that Jesus revealed.

God demanded righteousness. Jesus supported the demands of His Heavenly Father. From the beginning of His ministry, He demanded that the people should repent (make transformations in behavior that turned them from paths of unrighteousness to paths of righteousness). Almost everyone considered the religious leaders, the Pharisees and Sadducees, to be the most righteous people within their culture. The Pharisees and the Sadducees were not men to disagree with the people on that subject. However, these religious leaders were the people Jesus compared to snakes and whitewashed tombs. Those who saw themselves as the most righteous people, Jesus saw as among the most unrighteous. Their perception of reality and Jesus' perception of reality was opposite by 180 degrees.

The closer we study the words of Jesus, the more obvious it becomes that virtually every facet of Jesus' perception of good and evil was opposed to that of the people of the first century and of the world's population of the twenty-first century. As a prophet of Jehovah, he set out to change the hearts of humankind—to change all societies of the whole world—one person at a time.

He began where He was—in Galilee.

Early, in Jesus' ministry, He began with a message similar to that of John the Baptist. He began calling for repentance. He demanded a change in the hearts of His people. He still does.

Jesus Called for the People to Repent

When Jesus called for His people to "repent," He implied that people were going in the wrong direction. He was implying that those needing to repent are walking in the kingdom of Satan, away from the way of God. They need to turn to walk in the way of God, into a new kingdom—His Kingdom. Repentance is often misinterpreted to mean, "to feel regret for one's sin." It is that and more. Repentance requires a change of will, a change of volition, a change of purpose, and a change from the leadership of one lord to the leadership of another—the King of the Kingdom of God (of Heaven). Those He called needed conversion before they could enter.[6] They even needed to be born again, from above.[7]

Of course, this clearly stated that the rebirth was more than an action on the part of the individual. It included a miraculous action on God's part.[8] The Apostle Paul elaborated on this fact several years later when he wrote, "For by grace are ye saved through faith; and that not of yourselves: it is the gift of God: Not of works, lest any man should boast."[9] Repentance resulting in conversion results in a change of behavior, of spirit, of purpose, and of attitude. Despite the fact that virtually no one wants to hear that he or she is doing anything wrong, "Jesus began to preach, and to say, repent: for the kingdom of heaven is at hand."[10] Citizenship was available for all who would submit to His invitation to be ruled by the King of the Kingdom of God. Citizenship in other kingdoms was usually demanded in the face of force. However, Jesus only issued an invitation. He forced none.

But he warned that if they did not accept His rule, they were certain to be destroyed. Neither He nor the Father would destroy them, they would

---

6 cf. Mt. 18:3.

7 cf. Jn. 3:3.

8 cf. Mk.10:25f; Lk. 18:25.

9 Eph. 2:8-9.

10 Mt. 4:17.

destroy themselves.[11] Therefore, He pled with his hearers to repent. He was concerned with the best interests of each person He encountered. He appealed with love—never with violence. Not only was this not the style of other kings, such as Alexander the Great who was merciless with those who resisted his rule but even kind to those who swore allegiance to him. It was not the style of some leaders of the world's great religions.

When Muhammad came on the scene six hundred years after Jesus, as a warrior attacking caravans and leading Medinans in attacks against Mecca, prisoners had a choice. They could embrace Islam, or they would be slain.[12] We must admit that they for most people they employed an effective method of persuasion.

When men whom Jesus led began to repent, they were beginning to change their society, one person at a time. When Jesus sent His disciples out to preach among the people, He told them also to tell the people that they must repent.[13] He threatened no one. He forced no one. His disciples were to work to change the world one person at a time by introducing them to the way of their Lord. *Citizenship requires a commitment to abide by the laws of the Kingdom.* When Jesus clarified the conditions for citizenship in the Kingdom of God, He said, "Not every one who says to me, Lord, Lord, will enter into the kingdom of heaven,

---

11 Jn. 3:16-17 & Rom. 6:23.

12 Ishaq, p. 7.

13 cf. Mk. 6:12.

but he who does the will of My Father who is in heaven"[14] (Emphasis mine.)

The Supreme Commander Gives the Supreme Command

The Pharisees were accustomed to working to meticulously obey the Law given by Moses, but avoided the deeper intent of the law. Jesus filled that gap. He clarified. "A new commandment (law) I give to you, that you love one another; as I have loved you." The original Law had commanded them to love one anther.[15] However, Jesus had tacked on a profound phrase. He announced that citizens of the Kingdom of God must love as He loved! That required that citizens of the Kingdom of God must work consistently and habitually in the best interests of others.

It required that citizens were to love even their enemies. In centuries gone by, God had told his people what to do. Jesus told them how to do it and then demonstrated how to do it everywhere he went. When Jesus commanded the citizens of His kingdom to love, He was familiar with at least four words in His vocabulary for love that He could have used. He could have used a form of the word *storge* which is a word describing the love relationship between parents and children. He could have used a form of the word *phileo* which describes the love relationship between brothers, between sisters, between brothers and sisters,

14 Mt. 7:21 NKJB.

15 cf. Lev. 19:18.

and love between intimate friends. He could have used a form of the word *eros* which relates to sexual love. This form of love acts in anticipation of personal gratification. This word is not used in the New Testament.

Love as Jesus Taught It

Instead of any of these three, Jesus chose the word *agapé* when He commanded His subjects to love. Contrary to the other forms of love, this form of love has little or no feeling associated with it.

The *agapé* form of love essentially is a way of behaving. Therefore, it is largely visible. Instead of action based on feeling, it is action based on a decision. If I see that you have a need, *agapé* requires that I act to help fulfill that need. This form of love works in the other person's best interests. It helps. It encourages. It supports. All is without motive for personal gain. If I hold this form of love, I act in your best interests simply because you are you. With the *agapé* form of love, knowingly, I will do nothing to you, with you, or for you that is not in your best interest.

With this form of love in mind, Jesus, on another occasion said, "Do unto others as you would have others do unto you."[16] The *agapé* form of love made the citizens of His Kingdom into a community of servants. They were expected to serve their King by serving those whom the King loves. (You may be a parent. If someone does something good for your son or daughter, they

16 cf. Matt. 7:12.

do something good for you.) When citizens of His kingdom serve others, they serve the King.[17] What this strange contender for Kingship asked of others, he also did. He taught others to love—to work in the best interests of others, and He did as He taught others to do.

Some religious leaders have taught their followers to behave in one way but have acted in another. According to one of Muhammad's original biographers, Muhammad preached compassion and mercy, but sometimes acted cruelly.[18] Whereas Muhammad taught that war was a sacred duty demanded by Allah, Jesus taught love that required forgiveness.

Love even your enemies

Few things that Jesus said could have flown in the face of the people who heard Him more than His statements, "Ye have heard that it hath been said, Thou shalt love thy neighbor, and hate thine enemy. But I say unto you, Love your enemies, bless them that curse you, do good to them that hate you, and pray for them which despitefully use you, and persecute you; That ye may be the children of your Father which is in heaven."[19] Love our enemies? Do them good? The religion that Jesus promoted had the potential for profound change in the society in which He lived and beyond.

---

17 cf. Matt. 25:40.

18 Ishaq, p.9.

19 Matt. 5:43-45.

All their lives His people had lived by "an eye for an eye and a tooth for a tooth," as much of the world still lives today. For more than 2000 years, the culture of the entire Mediterranean world had taught them to retaliate. After another 2000 years, it still does. Instead, Jesus told his listeners, *Ye have heard that it hath been said, An eye for an eye, and a tooth for a tooth: But I say unto you, That ye resist not evil: but whosoever shall smite thee on thy right cheek, turn to him the other also.*[20] In essence, Jesus was telling them to stop the "eye for an eye and a tooth for a tooth" nonsense that could result in an endless cycle.

Mahatma Gandhi has been credited with having said that those who live by "an eye for an eye and a tooth for a tooth" are destined to end their days blind and toothless. Retaliation always begets retaliation that begets retaliation. You may have read of the Palestinian-Israeli repeated tit-for-tat warfare in today's newspaper. It has gone on for years with no end in sight.

Jesus said that citizens of His kingdom should forgive.

Love requires forgiveness

In forgiveness, the offended cancels the indebtedness created by the offender. Forgiveness makes no payback. Still wanting that which was best for His people, Jesus wanted no violence, warning that those who live by the sword are likely

---

20 Matt. 5:38-39.

to die by the sword.[21] And citizens of the Kingdom of God are expected to forgive time and time again. When Jesus' disciple, Peter came asking if he was expected to forgive an offender as many as seven times, Jesus told him to forgive, not only seven times, but seventy times seven—time after time after time.[22]

Those who heard Him would have responded, "What kind of kingdom does He want to establish? Forgive? Forget it! I will retaliate as my forefathers have done for thousands of years.

Jesus' listeners must have been even more startled when He said that the forgiveness of God for their sin was dependent on their forgiveness of others for their offenses. "But if you do not forgive others their trespasses [their reckless and willful sins, leaving them, letting them go, and giving up resentment], neither will your Father forgive your trespasses."[23] They did not want to hear those words any more than we want to hear them. (In more than seventy years of participating in public worship, I have never heard a sermon from that text.) They wanted to believe that if they offered their sacrifices, God would forgive their offenses, regardless of how many grudges they carried against others. This must have been another of

---

21 cf. Mt. 26:52.

22 Coincidental to the writing of this paragraph, in the background I heard on a TV program, "Forgive? Like Hell! I'll never forgive him!" The teachings of Jesus are as much the teachings of a maverick today as they were during His days as a young preacher in Galilee.
cf. Matt. 18:21-22.

23 Matt. 6:15 AB.

Jesus' "hard, offensive sayings" that caused many of His followers to say, "Who can be expected to listen to such teachings?"[24] These resisted the change demanded by His teachings. The cost of discipleship for them and their society was too much.

He had more "hard sayings." One of the Ten Commandments had prohibited adultery. For untold ages, men have smiled and said, "It's OK to look as long as I don't touch." But Jesus warned, *"Everyone who so much as looks at a woman with evil desire for her has committed adultery with her in his heart"* (Matt. 28). He even stated that citizens of His kingdom should guard against idle, meaningless chatter in conversation. Once again, He may as well have been saying that we must be perfect. Since we cannot do that by our own actions, we must depend on the King's grace of forgiveness that keeps us upright in His sight.

In the Law given to Moses on Mt. Sinai, God had made clear His concern for interpersonal relationships. Dan was required to forgive Justus. However, if Justus held a grudge against Dan, and Justus did not offer forgiveness to Dan, Dan was obligated to seek reconciliation with Justus. *"If when you are offering your gift at the altar you there remember that your brother has any [grievance] against you, leave your gift at the altar and go. First make peace with your brother, and then come back and present your gift."*[25] Jesus'

24 Jn . 6:60 AB

25 Mt. 6:23-24 AB.

concern for relationships among the citizens of His Kingdom emphatically included the relationship between husbands and wives. The divine ideal from the beginning had been for one man and one woman to remain together and not until death were they to part. Jewish law permitted divorce only by the husband. However, if the woman had strong grievance against her husband, she could petition the Sanhedrin who had the authority to force her husband to divorce her.

Instead of divorcing, Jesus wanted the alienated husband and wife to enjoy living in harmony.[26] He wanted them reconciled. Jesus knew that the *agapé* form of love that He commanded of the citizens of His Kingdom is the only love that keeps a man and a woman enjoying their relationship throughout the years of their lives. When the husband practices a lifestyle that steadily works in his wife's best interests, and the wife practices a lifestyle that steadily works in her husband's best interests, both come out ahead, and they enjoy life together. They want to remain together—not because they are forced to do so by some law. They want to remain together because they enjoy doing so. The *agapé* form of love had other implications.

Although Jesus did not directly attack the practice of slavery, no force in history has had as great an impact against slavery than the words of Jesus that commanded *agapé,* the form of love that works consistently in behalf of other

---

26 cf. Mt. 5:31-32; Mt. 19:8.

people. Indeed, His emphasis on love (*agapé*) was additionally revealed in His instructions to, "Do unto others as you would have others do unto you."[27] This form of love made the citizens of His kingdom into a community of servants, in which each citizen is to serve the others. He taught that they were expected to serve the King by serving those whom the King loves. Eldridge has appropriately written,

> It was not the purpose of Christ to overthrow the existing governments and social and political institutions by physical force; but through the power of truth, allied with human conscience, reason and conviction to so transform human character that such reforms and movements would be initiated, according to the needs and conditions of society, which in time would eradicate all wrongs, injustices, and cruelty among men.[28]

A worn adage says, "Actions speak louder than words." Jesus lived what he taught. In every way, He lived by the words He spoke. He showed no evidence of selfish desires, and He deceived no one at any time. He harmed no one, but He habitually worked in the best interests of all He met. Even when He was verbally abused, lied about, and physically assaulted, He showed no sign of hostility—even praying for His Heavenly Father to forgive those who were crucifying Him.

27 Matt. 7:12.

28 Eldridge, p. 25

Jesus' Closest Followers Became Changed Men

While Jesus preached and taught, healed the blind and lepers, and even raised the dead, a small group of men watched and listened. They were ordinary, hard working Jews. Only one was a "white collar worker." As Jesus got to know them better, He realized that they were weak men. One was overconfident, and impetuous—prone to speak before thinking. One was a skeptic. One was more concerned with money than with people. Two hungered for prestige. None cared enough about Him to offer comfort in the hours before He would be convicted of a capital crime and crucified. Judas betrayed Him, but instead of seeking forgiveness, in the courtroom of his own soul, he tried himself, declared himself guilty, deserving death by hanging. Similar to people of all generations, he worked to get for himself that which he felt he deserved.[29] During his trial, Peter denied even knowing him and then joined his peers who cowed fearfully in hiding behind locked doors.

Then the dual powers behind their religion and the government executed the man they had expected to become their king. They crucified Him. Those who had been closest to Him despaired in grief. Then something happened that transformed those ordinary men into bold spokesmen for God. **Their dead leader, Jesus, arose from the dead.**

---

29 Justice, 2008, *Damned if We Are Not Forgiven: Understanding Guilt and People Who Are Their Own Worst Enemies.*

For the next forty days, they talked with Him, shared meals with Him, and listened while He spoke to hundreds who would listen to what He had to say about the Kingdom of God. He was alive!

Without training or experience as public speakers, these emboldened men began to share their experiential knowledge of what He had said and of the fact that He had risen from the dead. They began preaching of that which they had seen and heard during the period of roughly three years that they had lived with Him—but always emphasized by the fact that He had risen from the dead.

They were so convinced of the utmost importance of their message and of the fact that He had come back alive after having been executed that they were willing to stake their lives on it. Separating and going in different directions, in keeping with Jesus' instructions, they began in Jerusalem, then fanned out into Judea, and then into the "uttermost parts of the world."

But people in those regions into which they traveled already had their gods. When some began to listen and believe the message delivered by those first Christian missionaries, the local religious leaders became outraged. Those men who were igniting fires of belief in the resurrected Christ would not keep quiet. They had to be silenced—executed. Tradition and legend tells us that all of those early followers of Jesus, except John, were executed by local religious authorities in the lands where they preached. Men do not give up their lives for a fabricated tale.

James, Jesus' half brother, was clubbed to death, and James the son of Zebedee was beheaded—both in Jerusalem. Matthew is believed to have died by the sword in Ethiopia. Mark was dragged to death by horses in Egypt. Religious leaders hanged Luke in Greece and Andrew was crucified in Greece. Peter was crucified in Rome and outraged religious men beat Bartholomew to death in Turkey. Thomas, the most reluctant to believe that Jesus had arisen from death was so convinced that Jesus truly had risen that he was willing to die in India because of his message. He was stabbed to death. Angry men had to shoot Jude with arrows from a bow to quiet him. Religious leaders where so upset because of the impact that Metthias was having on the people that they stoned him to death and then beheaded him. (Recall that this was the man who replaced Judas Iscariot.) Men are not willing to die for stories they have fabricated. They knew that they served a risen, living Savior. Lives were transformed—revolutionized—wherever they carried their message.

Principles of Jesus Ignited World-Wide Revolutions

When Jesus had come inviting, but never forcing men to become citizens in His new Kingdom, he set in human minds a form of government destined to influence societies around the world for millennia to come. He established in human minds the philosophy of government that granted the **right of the ruled to select their ruler.** This Christ—this Messiah—this King granted every person the privilege of surrendering to His rule or the privilege of continuing under the rule of the ultimate force of evil. Once the human race tasted the concept, the course of human history changed forever. News of bloodshed in efforts to claim the right of the ruled to select their ruler is as fresh as this morning's television news report.

Jesus' Execution: the Greatest Influence on World-Wide Social Change

After all else that He had said and done, Jesus' surrender of His life to be taken by crucifixion became the most important event in His life. That event coupled with His resurrection was destined to lead to the change of societies around the globe. The religious/psychological power of His vicarious death for the sins of humankind has enabled the hearts of hundreds of millions to permit themselves to be transformed; resulting in the transformation of entire societies. The people took on dual citizenship. They remained citizens of the lands of their nativity but they became citizens of the Kingdom of God—viewed by many as their conversion to Judaism.

For the first two hundred years, the movement established by Jesus was viewed as one more religious party within Judaism, differing from the Pharisees, the Essenes, and the Sadducees.

At various times, they were called Nazarenes, People of the Way, and Christians. Having begun in Jerusalem, citizens of the Kingdom of God moved on to Judea, and Samaria, and on toward the uttermost parts of the world. Some went specifically for the purpose of carrying the good news of the Kingdom of God. Some simply traveled with the wanderlust that has characterized much of the human race throughout history. Still others moved on to avoid persecution. To this day, wherever Christians have integrated into a society their efforts have led to changes that have improved the quality of the society.

Chapter 3

Christianity Began to Change Europe

Within only a few years after Jesus' crucifixion and resurrection, those who had accepted Him as their Lord—as their King were initiating so much change in their society that they were accused of "turning the world upside down" (Acts 17:6). However, able to speak only from their own perspective, their accusers erred! From the perspective of Christians, God through the convicting power of the Holy Spirit and the re-creative power of the resurrected Christ was turning their world right side up!

Few people, if any, could have imagined the extent of change ahead when Jesus said "Behold, I make all things new." The Romans were worshipping hundreds of gods, with each household containing its own. After Caesar Augustus was declared to be a god following his death, succeeding emperors were accepted as gods worthy of worship. When the head of state is considered a god, disloyalty to the state is a disloyalty to the deity and any disloyalty to the deity is considered treason, punishable by death.[30] They were practicing abortion, infanticide, glorifying homosexuality, and degrading their women. Early Christianity condemned such behaviors, pricked consciences, and was becoming responsible for initiating the transformation of thousands of the lives that would ultimately grow into the transformation of multiplied millions. Not one would have been transformed if Jesus had remained in the tomb.

Christianity Reduced Abortions and Infanticide

Abortion was the accepted method of birth control. Childlessness was considered a virtue and a woman without a child was more eligible than a woman with a child.

Writers of the period have concluded that "infanticide was infamously universal."[31] Infants were routinely killed soon after birth; usually by drowning. The sickly and the deformed had no chance. Roman law required it. Female infants

---

30 In the Gospels, we read that Pontius Pilate was hesitant to crucify Jesus, who had repeatedly proclaimed the Kingdom of God. After examination of Jesus, Pilate did not see him as a political threat. But then a member of the mob cried out, "If you release Jesus, you are no friend of Caesar's!" Pilate knew that at least one tattle-tail was likely to go straight to Rome to inform the emperor that a man called Jesus of Nazareth was promoting himself as a king and that Pilate was tolerating him. Pilate knew that the Emperor even supported professional informers. Pilate, fearful of losing his job and of severe punishment by the emperor was virtually forced to execute Jesus by crucifixion, the Roman method of execution of political prisoners.

31 Schmidt, p. 49.

were so commonly killed that the practice was considered responsible for the decline of Roman population early in the third century. The poet, Euripides wrote of infants who had been thrown into rivers, manure piles, and given as prey to the birds and beasts of the forests. Early Christians loudly condemned such behavior as totally lacking the kind of love that had been preached by their Lord. Not only did they condemn the abandonment of infants, they took many of them into their own homes and reared the children as their own. Before the influence of Christianity, infanticide was also common in Africa, China, India, Japan, and among the natives of North America, the Brazilian jungles, and the Eskimos.

Writings of the second century reveal no sign of guilt feelings by those who killed their children outright or by those who simply abandoned them in some desolate location to die or to be adopted and reared among animals. A moral conscience had not developed. (And unthinking people still ask, "Why did or does the world need a Savior?") Numerous stories and stage plays circulated that told of children who had been found and adopted into homes and of others who survived as feral children. Christians caught the attention of their non-Christian neighbors. Endowed by compassion encouraged by their Lord who had encouraged care for widows and orphans, by the middle of the second century AD, offerings were being taken among the churches for the care of orphans who were cared for in private homes.

By 333, the transforming power of Christ in the life of Constantine led to a law that required punishment for a father guilty of killing his son.[32] That was, indeed, a change.

During the first two centuries of the Christian era, hoards of uncivilized bands roamed the uncultivated regions beyond the Danube and on to the Rhine. Teutonic tribes were soon joined by other invading uncivilized people—Huns, Fins, Tartars, and Avars. Christianity, with its moral and ethical values slowly transformed the peoples as the religion of the resurrected, living re-creative Christ inched northward toward Britain. Even during the early centuries of the first millennium, the world would have been a far different world if Jesus had stayed in the tomb.

Life expectancy had been only about thirty since before the birth of Jesus. Mothers often died in childbirth and disease killed both mothers and fathers, often leaving infants and small children without a parent for support, protection, or leadership. Instead of being killed or abandoned, after Christianity became legalized by Constantine in AD 313, those children too young to fend for themselves were taken in and cared for in group homes. These were the first orphanages. Those Christian homes for children soon numbered more than 800. By the Middle Ages, many monasteries also were caring for orphaned children. Pagans marveled. Then they began to admire the Christians.

---

32 Eldridge, p.33.

The murder and the abandonment of infants was diminishing. From early in the spread of Christianity the followers of Christ had been making such a difference that their reputation rapidly spread even to the heads of state.

To the dismay of many Christians in post-Christian America, life has become cheap again. In recent years, millions of lives have been taken in institutions established for the purpose of killing helpless babies while still in the womb. A large percent of them have been executed by having their brains sucked out in the action known as "partial-birth abortions." Who but Christians would set up more than 3000 Crisis Pregnancy Centers in the U.S. that are helping pregnant women to find shelter and a home for their valued child after it is born? Even so, they cannot protect all children.

Other killers destroy the lives of small children who are simply playing in their yards in "drive by" shootings. Virtually, every parent in the United States lives with some sense of anxiety for the well being of their children who are in danger of being shot on the school ground or of being abducted, molested, and killed. The farther the nation moves from its Christian foundation, the closer it moves to lessening its value on human life. When Christianity fails to adequately change a society, the society degenerates and begins to replicate the most evil and Godless societies of the past.

Christians Cared for Widows and Orphans

Christianity was threatening the very foundations of the Roman Empire. Those early Christians who were "turning the world upside down" had to be silenced. Not only did they teach differently, they behaved differently. They spoke out against immoral practices. They respected women. They collected money to help care for widows and orphans. They had to be stopped. This led to persecution—sometimes by members of the general public in the regions in which Christians promoted the Gospel of Christ, but more often by the religious leaders of the pagan religions. Moreover, when the Christians were promoting citizenship in the Kingdom of God and rejecting worship of the emperor, Christians were charged with infidelity and disloyalty to the government.

Emperor Nero, after the great fire in Rome during July of AD 64 launched the most severe persecution against Christians up to that time. Many historians believe he was responsible for the fire and then blaming the Christians for having started it, he launched the persecution to divert rumors from himself. Roman governmental persecutions continued in varying degrees of intensity for roughly 200 years. Properties of Christians were confiscated, businesses destroyed, and thousands were executed. Still, Christianity continued to spread and to affect change in every society it infiltrated.

Christians Succeeded in Reducing Slavery

The Historian Gibbon estimated that in the first two centuries of the Christian era, sixty million slaves were held throughout the Roman Empire. Some have estimated more. Forty percent of the Italian peninsula was populated by slaves. The city of Rome numbered 500,000 slaves, so many that the citizens lived in constant fear of an uprising. For the same reason, the numbers were kept secret from public knowledge, fearing that if the slaves knew of their number, they would be more inclined to revolt.

More than three-fourths of all Athenians were slaves who performed all labor. The citizens of the Empire generally believed that work was beneath the dignity of their people. Slaves were given all work that ranged from that of the common labor to that of the most skilled craftsmen, creating a population of soft and worthless citizens of leisure. Slaves were made to do anything the owner asked of them. "Roman law gave absolute power to give, hire, sell, exchange, seize for debt, or kill a slave at his will."[33] Slaves could not own property, had no civil rights, nor did they have any legal standing in the courts. They were prohibited from marrying. Slavery was an affront to all Christian sensitivities. It violated virtually every value claimed by the slowly strengthening religion.

As Christianity spread within the Empire, Christians opposed the practice of slavery. With regenerated hearts, Christians were repelled by its

---

33 Eldridge, p. 21.

degradations of human life. They found support in the words of Jesus who commanded love *(agapé)* for one's fellow human beings and they found support in His teaching that told them to "do unto others an they wanted others to do to them" (cf. Matt. 7:12) "Christians proclaimed a gospel of emancipation from the darkness and slavery of sin into the truth and glorious liberty of the children of God. . . Christianity exalted gentleness, obedience, humility, patience, forgiveness, and love (*agapé*) for enemies—qualities which were despised by pagan freemen."[34] Christians knew that a change was needed.

It had not been the style of their Lord Jesus to wage violent crusades against social immoralities. Slavery was a social institution woven into virtually every fiber of Roman culture. Roman values were upside down. They needed to be uprighted. Social change is usually slow. By this time, in addition to the words of Jesus, the letters of Paul the Apostle were being circulated. After Jesus had ascended to the Father, Paul took the banner of Christianity and held it high. He told Philemon to regard his runaway slave, Onesimus, as a brother. Paul did as Jesus had done. He held the revolutionary position that Christians were to regard all people as equal before Christ. "Neither is there either Greek or Jew, slave or free . . . for you are all one in Christ Jesus" (Galatians 3:28). God's re-creative work in human life and His commandment to love as He had loved was

---

34 Eldridge, p. 24-26.

the foundation that was laid for a new world. The process of uprighting the upside down world was slow, but progress was being made. Major social change is rarely birthed full grown. Jesus had not directly attacked the social and political systems and His early followers recognized the wisdom that Jesus had demonstrated. Eldridge has again helped us understand the reasons.

> Christianity did not inaugurate a violent crusade against slavery. To have commanded and attempted the immediate overthrow of slavery in the Roman Empire would probably have wrought great havoc; brought greater burdens and suffering upon the unfortunate slaves, plunged masters and slaves into protracted war, and turned Europe and Asia into fields of blood. . . . Christianity proclaimed a gospel of emancipation from the darkness and slavery of sin into the truth and glorious liberty of the children of God, which was to lead without violence and bloody revolution to ultimate freedom from every form of bondage. The message rang out: The slave is your brother; he has a soul; he is a child of God; his life is sacred (p.25).

Without fanfare, Christians expressed their dismay to their friends and neighbors. But talk was cheap. By the second and third centuries, Christians had begun to set their slaves free.

Wealthy Christians began to purchase hundreds and then thousands of slaves—not to work them, but to free them—doing so publicly in churches by the leadership of the bishops. One man is known to have bought and freed 1400 slaves. Another freed 5000 and still another freed 8000 while others bought and freed as many as they could afford. Those who had little money contributed to funds collected for the purpose of purchasing and freeing slaves.

Of course, observers were astonished while the former slaves rejoiced in their newly discovered compassion among the Christians. Astonished by Christian compassion, multitudes of former slaves turned to Christ as their Lord. Those people with their strange new religion called Christianity did not behave as others did. They demonstrated love and compassion for all human beings. Love (*agapé*) among the loveless (those without *agapé*) stands out as a light stands out in darkness. Many slaves were accepting Christ as their Lord, becoming "Children of God" and "joint heirs with Christ." Christians accepted slaves as brothers and sisters. Christians, with their different lifestyle, were noticed and listened to.

With enlightened consciences, the Roman citizenry began to show respect for their slaves. Men who had the ear of men in power made their case for improving the lot of slaves. With an elevated cultural status, slaves were granted rights and were receiving more and more legal recognition. Favorable laws were enacted that made the lives of slaves more tolerable. Hadrian, AD 117-138, enacted laws that forbade the arbitrary killing of slaves, and the sale of slaves for "disgraceful purposes" was forbidden.[35]

By the time of Constantine (312-337) laws had been passed that greatly improved the lot of slaves. They could no longer be branded or crucified. Crucifixion of the slave seemed to show irreverence for the humble, crucified Christ. Two hundred years later, under Justinian (527-567) all privileges granted to citizens of the Empire were granted to emancipated slaves. Under Christian influence, marriage-ties between slaves became accepted as valid and indissoluble.

Even marriages between the free and the slave were recognized. Christian efforts to free slaves continued throughout Europe so that by the twelfth century slavery in Europe was rare, but traces of it continued until its revival in the early 1500s. By the end of that century, the slave trade between Africa and much of the rest of the Western World was flourishing[36] and would not end in England until Parliament finally prohibited it in 1833, following a long and weary struggle by William Wilberforce and his cohorts. Slavery continued in the United States of America until after the War for Southern Independence when the thirteenth amendment was signed in December of 1865.[37]

35 Eldridge, p. 27.

36 At that time, Africans already had been victims of slave trade for at roughly 2000 years.

37 Slavery continues to exist in some parts of the world.

Christianity Influenced Social Change at the Heart of the Roman Empire

By 300 Christianity was effectively represented in all parts of the Roman Empire.[38] Church Historian Williston Walker has written that Christianity was effectively impacting the empire on such a "significant scale" that many governmental officers and imperial servants were embracing Christianity. They had also penetrated the Roman army "on a considerable scale."[39] However, Emperor Diocletian tried to strip Christians from his armies and re-instituted intense persecution against Christians.

Rome experienced a rapid succession of emperors during the first decade of the fourth century. The empire was rapidly disintegrating into little more than a loose confederation of states. Under the rule of Galerius in April of 311, an edict was issued "tolerating Christians. . . on the condition that nothing is done by them contrary to discipline." When Galerius died in May of 311, the empire was "up for grabs" and to be ruled by the man who could lead the most powerful army.

Constantine's Influence

On October 28, 312 Constantine emerged the victor of the ensuing wars and Christianity had won the mind of Constantine. One of the greatest social changes in history was soon to follow.

38 Walker, p. 104.

39 Ibid p. 105.

He quickly issued the Edict of Toleration. Soon after that, Constantine issued from Milan an edict declaring complete freedom to Christianity. Christianity was no longer merely tolerated, nor was it declared to be the religion of the empire. It proclaimed absolute freedom of conscience, setting Christianity on a full equality with any religion of the Roman world, and even restored all properties that had been confiscated in the recent persecutions. Without strife, and without screaming for social change, the example set by Christians was making a difference in society.

Christians Cared for the Aged and the Disabled in Hospitals

The aged had been neglected for centuries. The sick were considered cursed by the gods. If the gods wanted sick people well they would get well without human intervention. Those who tried to intervene might be punished. Instead of permitting the continued neglect, even before Christians were granted new liberties by the government, Christians established homes (hospices – guest houses for the sick and chronically disabled) for the sick and aged. These seem to have been established in virtually every city into which Christianity had converted sizeable numbers and supported by Christian charitable donations. The first ecumenical counsel of the Christian Church at Nicaea in 325 directed bishops to establish a hospice in every city that had a cathedral. These early institutions were to nurse the sick, to provide shelter for the poor, and lodging for Christian pilgrims. The early nurses seem to have been women who were widowed, deaconesses, nuns, and monks of the church.

The first true hospital was built by St. Basil in Cappadocia about AD 369. Although history suggests that Brahministic medicine established a primitive hospital in the East as early as 431 BC, the concept did not reach the West until Christianity was maturing in the Roman Empire. Influenced by Jesus' concept of love as represented in His story of the Good Samaritan, they urged mercy and compassion on any neighbor in need and that any person in need was a neighbor. Roughly, 400 years later, impressed by Christian compassion for the sick, Arab Muslims began building hospitals in Arabic countries. Even Muslims had to respect Jesus as a great prophet. Christ was indeed a world changer.

Christians Give to Charities

The modern world accepts such institutions for granted, but evidence suggests that every orphanage, nursing home, assisted living facility, and hospital that exists on our planet today has at its roots the influence of Jesus Christ and those early Christians that were making a difference in every society they touched. Even those institutions that are so secular that they would never admit or even know of the social influence all bear the fingerprints of Jesus Christ and the movement He established that we call Christianity. All charitable institutions in the Western World have roots planted by Christ and His early followers. When one reads the New Testament writings of Paul the Apostle, the evidence is abundant that He repeatedly accepted financial offerings, not for himself, but for people who needed help because they were not able to help themselves. The strength of Christian charity is evidenced in the fact that studies have shown that church people give more than non-church people, not only to religious charitable organizations, but also to non-religious causes. Within two days after the great tsunami of 2004 hit Southeast Asia, the people of one Christian denomination alone had generously given $1,400,000 for disaster relief and within a month they had given more than $10,000,000. Not one penny was drained off for "Administrative Fees." One hundred percent was used to relieve human suffering. Many millions were donated by other Christian organizations.

Christian compassion continues to amaze non-Christians today as it has done from the first century. The influence of such charity has initiated change. Change tends to promote additional change.When one domino falls and strikes a second, that domino also falls and each succeeding domino knocks down the next. One can rarely see beyond the horizon to learn in advance of some changes that may be destined for the future.

Constantine Initiated More Change

From the efforts of Constantine, the Roman Empire could boast of one Emperor, one law, and one citizenship for all free men. By the time Constantine had enjoyed ruling for little more than a decade, he began to believe that the Empire should possess only one religion. By 319 the clergy were exempt from military service and obligations of the other well-to-do members of the society. Heathen sacrifices were also prohibited. Great churches were built at government expense in Rome, Jerusalem, and Bethlehem. By 321, Constantine decreed that Sunday was to be reserved as a religious holiday during which work was forbidden in the cities. The empire had become indisputably linked to the church and the church had become indisputably bound to the empire. Not by force of law, but by the social force of Christianity, the people were turning from the pagan gods.

Christianity Was Rapidly Triumphing Over Worship of Pagan Gods

Little more than a hundred years after Christ came forth from the tomb from death to life worship of Him was rapidly replacing the worship of the pagan gods. Tertullian, in his "*Appologia*" of the growth of Christianity wrote:

> We are but of yesterday but we have filled every place belonging to you, cities, islands, castles, towns, assemblies, your very camp,

> your tribes, companies, senate, forum. We leave you only your temples.[40]

The regression of polytheistic Roman worship and the progression of monotheistic Christian worship continued throughout the century, leading Clement of Alexandria to write,

> The word of our Master did not remain in Judea, as Philosophy remained in Greece, but has poured out over the whole world, persuading Greeks and Barbarians alike, race by race, village by village, every city, whole houses and hearers, one by one, nay, not a few of the philosophers themselves.[41]

The Greeks had formed the custom of chaining divine statues to their thrones to prohibit their escape. Roman conquers had helped them "escape." They believed that removal of a statue of a deity from a city removed its divine protection of that god. Therefore, Rome had become cluttered with the statuary of gods to worship.[42] One could never be too secure. The Olympian religion, with its many gods and myths had been dying for years. The incredible immoralities and violence among the gods had caused intelligent minds to question and doubt the religious beliefs that their ancestors had held for centuries. By the early fourth century, most people considered the tales

---

40 Eldridge, p. 18.

41 Eldridge, p. 19.

42 Graves, p. 57.

of the gods as shameful, laughable myths.

Constantine, who had once worshipped Apollo, the sun god, declared Christianity the official religion of the state in AD 337. Constantine's act served as the final death knell for the ancient religion.[43] Christianity was changing every society in which it was becoming accepted. History would later conclude that the joining of the church and state would prove both a blessing and a curse. God has often salvaged good out of the worst evils.

From the beginning of Jesus' ministry, steady change had resulted in every society His religion had touched. Gladiatorial games had been held in Rome for more than two and a half centuries before Jesus was born.

Christianity Ended Gladiator Contests

It is commonly believed that the first gladiatorial combat in Rome occurred when three pairs of gladiators fought to the death during the funeral celebration of Junius Brutus in 264 BC. However, some believe the gladiatorial games may have been held even earlier. During the prior three hundred years before Christianity was introduced in Rome, hundreds of thousands of gladiators had been publicly slaughtered in every conceivable manner. Dismemberment, disembowelment, and similar methods of mangling human bodies brought no tears but only cheers from those who watched for entertainment. That which virtually

43 Graves, p.11.

all the civilized world now thinks of as normal human repulsion to such carnage was unknown until Christianity was introduced to the world. We have good reason to think of Christ as the World Changer.

Similar to the way many other social changes were wrought by the influence of Jesus, Christianity dealt the decisive blow to the gladiator games. After Emperor Constantine made the new faith the Roman Empire's official religion, Christian critics of the gladiator games became more outspoken. Their denunciations echoed earlier reservations expressed by emperor Marcus Aurelius and by intellectuals Cicero and Seneca.

The Christian position was influenced, no doubt, by the experience of their own people in the arena. In earlier times, as a religious minority that did not recognize the Roman pantheon, Christians, like Jews, were easy targets of the powerful and the not so powerful alike. In addition to the gladiatorial combatants, thousands are believed to have died in Rome's Coliseum, burned alive, tied onto racks for lions or leopards to devour, or otherwise used as prey for the wild animal hunts that were an essential part of the games.

Social change is usually slow. The limitations on gladiators began slowly, but with great effect. In AD 200, women gladiators—always a source of debate, were banned from fighting. In 365, humans could no longer be thrown to wild animals; always a spectator high point. The imperial gladiator schools closed 34 years later but the grisly "spectator sport" continued.

In 404 AD, when spectators at the Coliseum killed a Christian named Tetramachus who had tried to stop a gladiator fight, Emperor Honorarius'[44] action was swift: he banned gladiator combat.[45] Christianity had struck down a six century old blight on a society. Other social change was rapidly in progress.

Christianity Reduced Sexual Immorality

Even the most casual student of Greek and Roman history is aware of the sexual immorality that pervaded during that period. Historian, Charles D. Eldridge has written, "Religious worship in pagan temples frequently made its sensual appeal and pandered to immorality. The worship of Venus, the goddess of fertility, promoted lewdness. . . Shrines to her were maintained at the expense of notorious courtesans."

Marriage had become without meaning. Every sexual perversion of which the human mind can contrive had become common practice among the people in their most humble houses and to the emperors in their most glorious bedrooms. Women copulated with virtually any available

44 Reigned 395-423

45 Popular legend has tied the Coliseum's gladiator games with the survival of Rome. In the years that followed Honorarius' ban, the city and arena both declined rapidly. Six years after the ban, barbarians sacked Rome. Eighteen years later, the Colosseum was damaged by an earthquake. Fifty-one years later, vandals sacked the city again. Just over 71 years after Honarius's gladiator ban, the last Roman emperor was deposed and the Roman Empire came to an end.

male and men copulated with virtually every available female. Every variation of group sex acts had become common.

However, Christian morality, with its Jewish background supported by the teachings of Jesus cried out against the sexual indulgences. Christians forbade fornication and adultery. To Christians, the sex act was confined to marriage between one man and one woman. Evidence of Christian morality began to prick and awaken the collective conscience of the people. The Christian message was slowly penetrating the hearts and minds of individuals. The greater society began to develop a sense of morality that led to one of the greatest social revolutions in history. Edward Gibbon wrote that "The dignity of marriage was restored by the Christians." When Christianity had changed enough people the whole society changed, preparing the way for still further change.

Christianity Elevated the Status of Women

Few North Americans seem to be aware of Christianity's influence that has elevated the status of women. Even fewer would doubt that "women's rights" have yet to attain a truly equal status with their masculine counterparts. However, even the privilege of fighting for equal status with men is the results of Christianity's influence on the society in which we live. It was at the heart of the ancient Greek and Roman societies that Christianity struck its early blow to the degraded position of women. Everyone (except the women?) knew that women were inferior to men. The typical woman had the social status of a slave. As a child, she was not permitted to attend school. After she had married she was forbidden to go out unless accompanied by her husband or trustworthy male escort; usually a slave appointed by the husband. She was never to interact with the husband's male guests. She could not speak in their presence, nor was she permitted to eat with them. Never was she permitted to speak in public. She was subject to public beatings for any violation of her husband's desires. (A friend once told me of the dismay he experienced in Islamic ruled Bahrain when he frequently watched women beaten mercilessly on the open streets for some minor infraction of their husband's will.)

With few exceptions, wherever Christianity has not been strongly accepted into the society, women continue to hold a low status. As in ancient Rome, women's primary purpose is assumed to be for the sexual pleasure of men and to bear their children.

The lot of Jewish women was little better than that of other women of the ancient Mediterranean world. Of course, women were not used sexually in the people's worship of Jehovah, but women were not permitted to speak publicly, nor were they worthy to testify in court. Indeed, women's voices were never to be heard in public when among men. She would have been shamed for doing so. Women were not to be heard singing in the synagogue until the late 1700s. Jesus had the ingenious ability to attack major social evils by implication and demonstration instead of by caustic attack. As He assailed the practice of slavery by preaching love for one another, in the same way, He fought against the common attitudes and practices that diminished the value of women.

Even the most casual reading of the four Gospels makes clear that Jesus respected women and women respected Him. Always the maverick, refusing to live by the traditions of His people, Jesus respected women and worked to elevate their position in society. I can say it no better than Alvin Schmidt, "His actions and teachings raised the status of women to new heights, often to the consternation and dismay of his friends and enemies. By word and deed, he went against the ancient, taken-for-granted beliefs and practices that defined women as socially, intellectually, and spiritually inferior."[46]

When He met "the woman at the well" in Samaria, He violated tradition by speaking to her—even in a public place. According to rabbinic law, He brought disgrace upon Himself by stooping so low as to publicly converse with a woman. Even His disciples were surprised to find Him talking with a woman (cf. John 4:5-29).

On another occasion, when visiting in the home of Mary and Martha, He again violated rabbinic law by teaching a woman: Mary. Women

---

46 Schmidt, p. 102.

were assumed to be too stupid, and unworthy of religious instruction. Mary would have felt privileged to be taught by virtually any man. However, to be taught by the itinerant rabbi, she would have felt especially grateful and privileged. (cf. Luke 10:38-42)

After Jesus' resurrection from death, He chose women to be the first carriers of the good news (gospel). He could just as easily have chosen Peter and John (cf. Matt. 28:10). Because of Jesus' respect for women, they were among His most admiring followers. He could not have permitted them into the small inner circle of his disciples that traveled throughout Galilee and into Samaria and Judea. He had to remain above a suspicion of immoralities, and He had to protect the reputation of the men who traveled with Him.

When some of his countrymen were eager and willing to stone a woman to death because she had been caught in an adulterous act, Jesus was even more eager and willing to forgive her and to encourage her not to return to such destructive and degrading behavior. It seems no wonder that women were attracted to Him. Women throughout the ages have been attracted to men who are kind and gentle, protective, forgiving, and wanting that which is best for them.

He carried no banner and preached no sermons on the dignity and worth of women. He created no "women's rights movements. Instead, He let His actions, His attitude, and His message of repentance, of salvation, and of the kind of love that acts in other people's best interests follow its natural course. That course would lead whole societies to the most profound respect for women that the world had yet known. And women have responded positively for the past 2000 years.

Even they became evangelists and missionaries as exemplified by Phoebe and Priscilla. Women commonly were more active in the early church than men, and church historians have long recognized that across the ages, women more than men have been responsible for the church's growth. Every pastor knows that without the women of the modern church, much of the best ministry by virtually every church would have died long ago. The church is blessed by the fact that to this day, women are more attracted to Jesus and His church than men.

Five centuries had passed since Christians had begun making gigantic changes among the Southwestern Europeans. (This is roughly, the same amount of time between the arrival of Christopher Columbus on the North American continent and our modern day.) The Roman Empire had ended in 475 with defeat by the Goths.[47] Event influenced event as dominos knock down dominos. Christian influence had steadily increased.

Christian Influence Diminished

Warring Factions

Small, but bloody private wars were sanctioned

47 Historians probably will never cease to debate which date to establish as the actual end. This date is close enough for our purpose here.

by the tribal gods of war during the early centuries of the Christian era in Western Europe. Private wars brought frequent loss of life and property. Any man who believed himself wronged was inclined to declare war against his enemy. Kinsmen who refused to join the war lost clan relationships advantages. Plunder and bloodshed was rampant. Towns and tribes not involved in the fight were often "caught in the crossfire." Crops were frequently destroyed, cattle were driven off, cities were laid waste, and society was torn by strife after strife.

On the scene migrated a weird people called Christians who roamed the countryside, where they found listeners in private homes and audiences in the villages. They heralded a message emphasizing not only the re-creative power of God in human life, but they pled for the "Peace of God." Christian clergy led leagues and associations of peace that sought to end the waste of life and property in the private wars. Men listened and heeded the proclaimed "Truce of God." In response, leading barons of war signed pacts of peace and assigned heavy penalties to the violation of the oath of peace. Even those who had not signed a pact could suffer the consequences for entering personal feuds. The peace movement continued to spread through Europe even into the twelfth century. Christianity was becoming the uniting bond among the people of Europe.

Christianity Changed the Arts

Painting and Sculpture

Something basic in human nature longs to express itself in pictures. From the earliest known inhabitants on earth, the people expressed themselves and communicated something of their world to be interpreted in millennia that followed. Even the small child begins early to draw images representing what he or she sees. Some of the earliest art in Christian burial chambers still tell something of the concerns of the people.

The world's greatest art collections would look far different if Jesus had remained in the tomb. How void the world's great museums would look without the genius of Leonardo da Vinci, Botticello, Michaelangelo, Titan, Giotto, Raphael, and many other great artists of profound religious conviction and devotion. I envision the blank canvases hanging where their magnificent paintings now hang and empty platforms and pedestals where supreme sculptured figures now stand.

Architecture

I envision empty lots and little shops built on the grounds where the world's magnificent cathedrals now stand and beautiful Roman edifices and statues of pagan gods where now stand the architectural contributions of Christian influence. Early, in the second millennium, "Bishops and monks devoted time to the study of architectural science, and artists of Italy, Germany, and France gave freely of their genius and innovative ability" to architectural marvels such as the world had never before seen.[48]

Music

Not only was Christianity responsible for changing the arts of architecture, painting, and sculptured figures, Christianity has had its influence in music. From the earliest times, human beings have used the widest variety of things available to create forms of music. Archeological evidence places the flute, stringed instruments, and the drum as instruments of musical interests among some of the world's most ancient people. It seems easy to assume that the human voice echoed among the recesses of the earliest cave dwellings. The most ancient Mesopotamians, Chinese, Egyptians, Greeks, Romans, Hebrews, South Americans, Mesoamericans, and North Americans all invented their own methods of making sounds that were music to their ears. The earliest Christians followed the practice of associating music with their worship.

However, it was not until the fourteenth or fifteenth century that counterpoint was developed. This made possible for the first time the enriched blending of several independent parts in which human voices and multiple musical instruments produced harmonious pleasing melodies. Within a century, Christian men such as Mozart, Hayden, and Beethoven were recognized by kings, popes, bishops, and the listening ears of the general

---

48 Eldridge, p.133

public for their contributions to music worthy of use in the worship of God.

In more recent centuries, Christian Negroes of the slave period in North America developed their "music of hope"—the Spirituals. Some music historians insist that the highly symbolic "Negro Spiritual" music of the antebellum period in North America was to that period as was the Biblical Book of the Revelation was to the downtrodden and despairing people of the first century. Not only was the "Spiritual" a distinctively Christian innovation, but from that music developed the musical style commonly known as "jazz." If Jesus had stayed in the tomb, the modern recording industry with its many styles of music that fill the preferences of millions of purchasers of sacred music would not exist.

Literature

If Jesus had remained in the tomb, some of the world's greatest literature would never have been written. The Bible would never have become the most published book of all time. Such classics as John Bunyan's *Pilgrim's Progress*, Milton's great works, *Paradise Lost* and *Paradise Regained*, would never have been written. The books, the poetry, and the fiction built on the Life of Christ could fill the greatest libraries. Shakespeare, Browning, Wordsworth, Shelly, Whittier, Wesley, Hawthorn, Spenser, and numerous other "name" writers would never have produced their most renowned works if Jesus had remained in the tomb.

Charlemagne Left an Indelible Mark on History

Charlemagne would hold a far different place in history if Jesus had stayed in the tomb. Charlemagne came to power in AD 771. "Perhaps more than any other sovereign in history, Charlemagne was head over all things of his age." He won rule over all of modern France, Belgium, Holland, Italy, Austria, Hungary, nearly half of modern Germany, and a portion of Spain. In 799, he took Brittany. On Christmas day of 800, Pope Leo III crowned him emperor of the Western (Holy Roman) Empire. "He quickly became known as the patron of learning, the kindly master of the church, and the preserver of order to whom nothing seemed too small for attention or too great for execution." He believed that government should be for the benefit of the governed—a rare philosophy held by rare men in any period of history.

Charlemagne's Legacy to the World

Charlemagne's conquest of the Saxons of Germany greatly influenced the societies of the era by forcibly imposing Christianity on the people who had embraced other gods or no god at all. He envisioned himself as the earthly head of the Kingdom of God.

Charlemagne became known as a tireless reformer who tried to advance his people's lot in many ways. He set up money standards to encourage commerce, tried to build a Rhine-

Danube canal, and urged better farming methods. He especially worked to spread education and Christianity in every class of people.

He well earned the title "Patron of Learning." At the time Charlemagne gained power, no schools in Western Europe compated with those that flourished in connection with the monasteries of the British Islands. Charlemagne continued to follow the Christian ethic that requires adherents to consistently work in the best interests of others. Only his harshest critics have denied that he believed in the philosophy that the government exists to serve the best interests of the governed, and that he worked to that end.

Although Charlemagne never gained the full allegiance of the people of the aisles of Britton, with the aid of Alcuin, a British scholar and ecclesiastic, he carried English learning back to the continent. There, Alcuin and other imported educators cultivated the best of British education in Charlemagne's Palace school. Preaching was encouraged and books of sermons were prepared. His efforts soon bore fruit by raising a generation of churchmen whose morals and whose education were of a higher standard than before. Even the most poorly educated Christians were able to repeat the Lord's Prayer and the Apostle's Creed. The die was thus cast that shaped Western European education for centuries to come.

Christians "invented" the university style of education. Earlier Romans had hired individual tutors for advanced studies, but never before the twelfth century had students been brought together in groups to follow prescribed courses of study that would lead to recognized degrees or certificates.[49] The university believed to be the first, the University of Bologna in Italy, was established in 1158. The second was founded in 1200 as the University of Paris. Modern universities continue their legacy in that they are known for their research. Even those first universities were involved in research that required intense study of ancient documents, but they did no empirical research. Their research was largely theological, and they set precedents for centuries to come.

> Through their monastic roots and through the nineteenth century, all universities were founded as Christian institutions regardless of whether they taught law, theology, or medicine. Until well into the nineteenth century, even with the growth of scientific studies, Western universities and colleges almost always operated within theological boundaries.[50]

Although the earliest university programs in theology, was created to train parish clergy, the degree of Bachelor of Arts was soon awarded in the fields of medicine, civil or Roman law for use primarily in Italy, and philosophy, the root of the modern Doctor of Philosophy degree.[51]

49 Spicknard, p. 98

50 George E. Marsden, *The Outrageous Idea of Christian Scholarship*, New York: Oxford University Press, 1997, p. 15.

51 Spicknard, p.99.

Many historians believe that Charlemagne's concern for education became his most significant contribution to the complex European society. Every great educational institution of the western hemisphere and their students continue to reap the benefits of Charlemagne who sought to obey the Great Commission (Matt. 28:19-20) of Jesus Christ. He wanted teachers to be qualified to teach by going even into the world of ignorance.

The Church in Conflict Weakened Christianity's Influence on Society

When Charlemagne died, his son, Louis the Pious, a much weaker personality than his father, was not up to the task of ruling in Charlemagne's stead. When Louis died after twenty-six years of feeble rule, the weakened Empire was divided by the Treaty of Verdun in 843 to be ruled by Louis' two quarreling, ineffective sons.[52] Without a strong central government, local seats of authority vied for superiority. Conditions were ripe for the development of a feudal system and for the strengthening of the papacy. Central rule of both, the state and religion had evaporated.

No one ruled the papacy. Parties arose that supported various men for that office. The following centuries were destined to be characterized by strife among men who vied for rule over the church and among men who vied for rule over the state. The eleventh century saw a period in

52 This is generally regarded as the point at which Germany and France became divided.

which three popes claimed to rule at the same time. The papacy became the sport of European nobles. Laypeople of the church were disgusted.

When the church does not influence the society, the society influences the church.

While the church was losing its credibility in the eyes of the people, the universities of Europe were flourishing. The period between 1409 and 1506 experienced the founding of no fewer than twelve universities. Having begun at the University of Vienna, godless Humanism rapidly became the accepted and promoted philosophy of life that was to continue in varying degrees of influence into the current millennium. Serious promoters of humanism seem to differ little in their definitions of its philosophy.

> Humanism is a rational philosophy informed by science, inspired by art, and motivated by compassion. Affirming the dignity of each human being, it supports the maximization of individual liberty and opportunity consonant with social and planetary responsibility. It advocates the extension of participatory democracy and the expansion of the open society, standing for human rights and social justice. Free of supernaturalism, it recognizes human beings as a part of nature and holds that values—be they religious, ethical, social, or political—have their source in human experience and culture. Humanism thus

derives the goals of life from human need and interest rather than from theological or ideological abstractions, and asserts that humanity must take responsibility for its own destiny. *The Humanist Magazine.*[53]

Some few brave souls began to oppose Godless humanism. Strong voices pointed less to the dogmas of the church and more to the words of their Bible. In 1436, a goldsmith named Johannes Gutenberg began to build a printing press with replaceable/moveable wooden or metal letters—an invention that many view as significant as the invention of the wheel. By 1440, Gutenberg's printing device was complete.

Christians Took Advantage of Gutenberg's Press

The church recognized its potential significance of Gutenberg's invention. By 1500, no fewer than ninety-two editions of the Vulgate translation of the Bible had been made available to the church. Eighteen editions of a German version were printed before 1521. Although efforts had been made to restrict the reading of the Bible, familiarity with it greatly increased among the less educated priesthood and among laymen. A problem, in its embryonic state, was already forming. Those who did not challenge the reliability of the Bible, recognized problems of interpretation that have characterized most disputes in the church since

53 http://www.americanhumanist.org

the earliest days of the church's existence.

At least as early as the ancient Persian Empire, various systems of mail delivery had made it possible for the writing and delivery of messages over thousands of miles. Museums cannot contain all of the multiplied thousands of clay tablets that archeologists have discovered and deciphered that were written in the regions of ancient Mesopotamia. For the next three thousand years, although the writing materials changed, the method of writing continued one letter at a time by human hands. (Even during Jesus' boyhood, every child was required to attend school where they were taught to read and write.[54]) Multiple copies were painstakingly made letter by letter. After Gutenberg invented his press, not only could the Bible be duplicated, but other writings also.

Revolutionary change could be promoted, not only by hand-written notes but by printed pamphlets and books. Some writers of the period promoted war against particular foes. But Christians accepted the maxim, "The pen is mightier than the sword." They wrote, had their words set in type, printed, and distributed to gain support for the causes in which they believed. They promoted social change without the shedding of blood. With these, they won the backing of hundreds and then of thousands. Of course this medium of communication was soon adopted by non-Christians also. Since the invention of the Gutenberg Press, sane men and

---

54 Justice (2004), p. 98.

women have continued to write, believing that "the pen is mightier than the sword." They have worked to promote bloodless social revolutions.

Martin Luther's Ministry Led to Church Split

Threat of attack by the Turks and the German famine of 1490 to 1503 made many believe that their land was under divine judgment. Perhaps God was angry and needed to be appeased. Viewing Christ as an angry judge, "intercession of Mary was never more sought, and Mary's mother, St. Anna, was but little less valued."[55]

Germany was threatened by war and the many believed that war would be an expression of God's judgment upon them. At the same time, the church was selling indulgences to raise monies for building the church of St. Peter in Rome. The people were liberally responding—expecting their time in purgatory to be shortened. In the wake of the opposition expressed by the religions teachings of a priest named Martin Luther, thousands split from the Roman Church and societies were changed for centuries to come; perhaps forever. Every Protestant has his or her roots embedded in that schism.

King Henry VIII Also Split from the Church of Rome

By the early sixteenth century, Henry VIII firmly ruled England while practically controlling

55 Walker, p. 333.

Episcopal appointments (appointment of Bishops) with the approval of the Pope in Rome. At the beginning of his rule, he had married Catherine of Aragon, the daughter of Ferdinand and Isabella of Spain. When Catherine could bear no male child who could succeed him to the throne, Henry conveniently "fell in love" with Anne Boleyn, a lady of his court, who would bear no sons, but a daughter, Princess Elizabeth; later to be Queen.

When Pope Clement VII refused to grant an annulment of the marriage between Catherine and Henry, other issues soon added to the tensions between Henry and the Pope. At convocations of clergy in 1531, Henry ably "persuaded" the body to announce that in respect to the Church of England, Henry was the "single and supreme Lord, and as far as the law of Christ allows, even supreme head."[56] Early in 1532 under Henry's pressure, Parliament approved an act that forbade payments of all annates (the large receipts of the church) to Rome except with the king's consent. The Pope threatened excommunication. Henry responded by pressuring Parliament to issue a series of statutes by which all payments to the Pope were to cease, all bishops were to be elected on the King's nomination, and all recognitions of papal authority abandoned.

In November 1534, the breech with Rome became complete when Parliament passed the Supremacy Act. Therein, Henry and his successors were declared as "the only supreme head in the

56 Walker, p. 403

earth of the Church of England." They added no qualifying clauses. The act denied all authority of the Pope in England and bestowed upon the king emoluments and revenues that had hitherto been paid to the see of Rome. In essence, the King had become the Pope of the Church of England and in concept, the role has continued into the twenty-first century. Some reports have surfaced alleging that Prince Charles, Prince of Wales and heir to the British crown, has said that upon coronation, he plans to renounce his kingly role as head of the Church of England.

Historians are left to debate whether the state of the early sixteenth century was affecting the society or the society was affecting the state. It seems more accurate to say that each was affecting the other.

In 1625, Charles I ascended the throne of England. Even while masses were abandoning England and its king, the people were being empowered by Parliament, and Parliament was being empowered by the people. A slow shift in thought among the people was reversing the political philosophy that had been held in prior centuries. The king was becoming answerable to the people through their representatives in Parliament. As Charles and Parliament clashed in words, they also began to draw parties around them who were willing to fight. Charles was the traditional head of the army, but Parliament held the greater resources. Charles' army gathered its forces at Oxford and Parliament gathered its citizen army at London. England was suddenly engulfed in a civil war. Charles attacked the army of Parliament in London, and Parliament retaliated with an attack on Oxford. To this day, virtually every building in the city of Oxford shows evidence of having been designed to defend against attackers.

After repeated attacks against one another, Parliament's forces captured King Charles. H. G. Wells, in his *Outline of History* stated, "The English were drifting towards a situation new in the world's history, in which a monarch should be formally tried for treason to his people and condemned."[57] When appeals were made that declared the king above trial by law, the Rump Parliament proceeded with the trial, declared him guilty, and ordered his execution by beheading. "The likes of it had never been heard of in the world before. Kings had killed each other before. . . but that a section of the people should rise up, try its king solely and deliberately for disloyalty, mischief, and treachery, and condemn and kill him sent horror through every court in Europe."[58] These events served as budding seeds of democracy as the people began to claim their right to choose their leaders and to hold their leaders accountable to the people.

As dominos topple dominos, events trigger further events. By the latter years of the sixteenth century, the Puritans had gained a strong niche

57 Wells, p.815.

58 Wells, p.816.

within the Church of England, and many of them were looking toward the New World.

Chapter 4

Christianity Quickly Changed North America

Presbyterian & Puritan Congregationalism Planted Seeds of Democracy

Presbyterians had gained strength in England, and Puritan men of the Church of England with backgrounds of learning in Zurich and Geneva saw in the Scriptures a clear pattern of church government distinctively different from that which existed in England. They were convinced that in the New Testament, the words "bishops," "presbyters," and "pastors" were synonymous. They saw no hierarchy among those who held spiritual offices. All were essentially equal. They began to seek the abolition of the offices of archbishops, and archdeacons, and the election of pastors by the people of individual churches. They insisted on essential spiritual parity among those in positions of spiritual leadership. The time was right for Robert Browne, of Cambridge, to set forth the principles of Congregationalism.

According to Browne, the only church is

> a local body of experiential believers in Christ, united to Him and to one another by a voluntary covenant. Such a church has Christ as its head, and is ruled by officers and laws of His appointment. Each is self-governing and chooses a pastor, a teacher, elders, deacons, and widows, whom the New Testament designates; but each member has responsibility for the welfare of the whole. No church has authority over any other, but each owes to the other brotherly helpfulness.[59]

The system set forth was essentially that of a democracy.[60] Some believe that Browne was strongly influenced by the thoughts of the Anabaptists who flourished in the earlier half of the century. These seeds of thought planted among the populace by men of religious faith were destined to change the course of world history. Those thoughts would continue to shake and reframe governments even into the twenty-first century.

In January 2000, the Freedom House organization counted 120 democracies. This was the highest number of democratic governments in the history of the world. This meant that sixty-three percent of the world's population was enjoying the freedoms of democracy; the largest

---

59 Walker, p. 461.

60 The word "democratic" means "rule by the people." It has often been said that democracy is "rule by the ruled."

percent in history.[61] The Christian religion has truly influenced the change of societies around the world.

The king was well aware of the mounting dissatisfaction. As the legal head of the church in England, the rising tide of thought that promoted democratic government inside the church or inside the government could not be tolerated. Promotion of democracy sounded treasonable. When efforts were made to silence the spokesmen, fires of anger kindled in the hearts of the people toward both the King and Parliament. The people grumbled loudly when the king silenced the pastors and canceled lectureships in the universities. Separatists had already sailed to the New World. Distressed by the religious and political outlook in England, Puritans began to join the Separatists in North America.

By 1628, imigration to Massachusetts had begun. The newcomers quickly established a church in Salem. With the arrival of even larger numbers, strong churches soon dotted the Massachusetts landscape. It was no form of abstract religious liberty that the people sought. They came to create a setting in which they had freedom of speech and could organize as they desired. Many were not even interested in the Separatist Movement fostered by many of their new fellow Christians. However, similar to the Separatists, they looked to the Bible as the sole law of the organization of their churches. To

---

61 http://www.hoover.org/publications/digest/3491911.html

them, this meant that their churches were to be organized on the Congregational model.

No longer with the mere seeds of a philosophy for government, the Puritans brought to the New World the growing saplings of a new democracy. By 1640, at least 20,000 Puritans had settled in New England. They wanted democracy in their churches and they wanted democracy in their government. Back in Europe, the news was spreading rapidly that the people who had gone to the New World were building a land where the people were free to worship or not to worship as they chose, and they were inclined toward a government in which the elected officials were considered servants of the people.

By the time men gathered in Philadelphia to draft the U.S. Constitution, 156 years after the first Pilgrims had landed in Plymouth, Massachusetts, more than three million men, women, and children had immigrated to North America, with Protestant Christianity as the dominant driving philosophical force.

Christian Education Laid Religious Foundations in North America

When the Pilgrims came to North America in December, 1620, they came with a charter for land in Virginia. However, instead of arriving in Virginia, they landed at Plymouth, Massachusetts. Before they disembarked the Mayflower, each person voluntarily signed a covenant agreeing to Christian self-government. That document became known as the Mayflower Compact. It read,

> In the name of God, Amen. We whose names are underwritten, the loyal subjects of the dread Sovereign Lord, King James. . . . Having undertaken *for the glory of God, and the advancement of the Christian Faith* and the Honor of our King and country, a voyage to plant the first colony in the northern parts of Virginia; do by these Presents solemnly and mutually in the presence of God and of one another, covenant and combine ourselves together a civil Body Politic, for our better Ordering and Preservation and Furtherance of the Ends thereof. (Italics mine.)

Those men and women felt fortunate when they were able to renegotiate the charter with authorities in London. This was among the things for which they gave thanks on that first Thanksgiving Day in 1621. They arrived only nine years after the King James Version of the Bible had been translated. After the Pilgrim's passion for religious liberty, their next greatest passion was their passion for education of their young so that they could read the Bible for themselves. More Puritan Christians were bound for the North American shores.

> In 1630, John Winthrop sailed on the Arbella, the flagship of eleven vessels loaded with more than a thousand Puritans

> seeking freedom to worship without threat of persecution. From the deck of the ship, before disembarking, Winthrop delivered a lay homily that he called "A model of Christian charity." In it he set down what he believed his people should intend for their new world. "Winthrop believed the Puritans should settle together in a city or town where large and small farmers and merchants alike would form a community housing their church, their government, and their defenses against enemies, whether Indian or European. He believed it would be a "city of God" and "a city upon a hill."[62] The Puritans would worship as the Bible intended them to. Men and women would aid each other, and as a consequence, serve God. . . . make other's conditions our own, rejoice together, mourn together, labor and suffer together. . . .[63]

Winthrop's message seems to have been somewhat similar to a coach's last minute talk before the "big game." Their "big game" held implications for centuries ahead. But within twenty years, delegates from all the new colonies signed the New England Confederation which read in part, "We all come into these parts of America with one and the same end and aim, namely, to advance the Kingdom of God of our Lord Jesus

62 Winthrop believed the new land should become a source of light to the whole world.

63 Butler, p. 32.

Christ."[64] When villages sprang up in the New World, the people wanted to establish schools as quickly as possible. In them their children could learn to read. Ministers had been taught to read in the schools back in Europe. By this time, some others had gained access to the European educational centers. If the village had a minister or someone else who could read, the village had a teacher—and most villages and towns had one or both.

No one objected to the Bible being taught in those early schools—even those few that were not church sponsored. A mere sixteen years after the Pilgrims first arrived in 1620 the Rev. John Harvard opened the College of New Jersey in 1636. He declared it as an institution for training "a literate clergy." Of course, that school was to become Harvard University. The original *Harvard Student Handbook* rule number one stated that students seeking entrance must learn Latin and Greek *so they could study the Scriptures.*

Also as church sponsored institutions, Yale opened in 1701, and Princeton opened in 1748. Gradually, these schools became the educational centers for educating teachers who would go on to establish some of the greatest educational systems the world had ever known. Christians founded the New World's first 126 colleges. Adhering to Judeo-Christian morals and values, they unapologetically used the Bible as the foundation of their teachings. The curricula of the period

64 Kennedy, p. 62.

were developed by a devout follower of Jesus Christ. That man, Noah Webster, became known as "America's school master." He was convinced that schools held the responsibility for teaching Christian moral values to children. Graduates of those great centers of education were blessed by being significant figures in further shaping the culture of the period.

Many historians believe that the great revivals from 1738 to 1760, commonly known as the Great Awakening, were preparing the colonists with the mental and moral fiber needed to declare independence from England. They needed mental and moral toughness, but they also needed the toughness that would help them prevail through the years of the Revolutionary War that rapidly was approaching.

Christians Built First Hospital in North America

Quakers had a reputation for trying to minister to the needs within the context of where they lived. The ill had no provision to meet their needs. A Quaker, Thomas Bond, a physician educated in England formed a partnership with another Quaker; John Fothergill decided to establish a hospital "for the cure of poor sick persons." With the support of Benjamin Franklin, also a strong supporter of Christianity, they built the first hospital on North American soil in 1751 in Philadelphia, Pennsylvania. This hospital then supplied the facilities for the first American medical school.[65]

Tensions between England and America had stressed to the breaking point. The British wanted to investigate reports that the colonists were stockpiling weapons in the Concord-Lexington region, a few miles west of Boston. On April 19, 1775, at about 4:30 AM, 600 British troops, assembled in battle lines, appeared in gleaming red and white uniforms with shiny brass buttons and buckles. About 70 American militiamen stood surprised when a Captain Parker yelled, “Stand you ground! If they want war, let it begin here!” And it did. The American men were regular townsmen, many owned property, but others were working men. Knowing they could not overpower the British forces with the tiny American group of men, Captain Parker ordered his men to disband, but the British commander Major Atcairn had orders to take the American’s weapons. A small skirmish arose between the Americans and British. Parker and seven others were killed. This, the Battle of Lexington, signaled the beginning of the American Revolution. Some have called it “the shot that was heard ‘round the world.”

Foundations Were Laid for the American Revolution

By the end of the twentieth century, with growing support that has continued into the current century, pseudo-intellectual secular humanists and atheists have been speaking so

65 Atken, et. al., p. 21.

loudly that it has become a popular belief that the United States of America was not founded by Christians, but by deists, atheists, humanists, and men addicted to the French Enlightenment philosophy. An elementary search of the World Wide Web will turn up numerous articles to that effect. They lie, or they parade their ignorance before the world. Such a thesis simply cannot stand up to the evidence available from readily available documents.

Men of Strong Christian Convictions Were Rising in Prominence

Modern Americans need occasionally to look at the lives of some of the men who led the colonists into the Revolution against England, thereby changing the American society forever.

PATRICK HENRY spoke words that virtually every school child has heard: "Give me liberty or give me death." But secular influences have failed to include in the textbooks the context within which he spoke those words. Often called a "firebrand of the Revolution," Patrick Henry said,

> "An appeal to arms and to the God of Hosts is all that is left us. But we shall not fight our battle alone. There is a just God that presides over the destiny of nations. The battle sir, is not of the strong alone. Is life so dear or peace so sweet that as to be purchased at the price of chains. Forbid it Almighty God. I know not what course others may take, but as for me, give me liberty or give me death."

Not a man of few words, he also said,

> It cannot be emphasized too strongly or too often that this great nation was founded, not by religionists but by Christians; not by religions, but by the Gospel of Jesus Christ! For this very reason peoples of other faiths have been afforded asylum, prosperity, and freedom of worship here.[66]

He later said,

> "I have disposed of all my property to my family. There is one thing more that I wish I could give to them, and that is the Christian religion. If they had that and I had not given them one cent, they would be rich. If they have that not, and I have given them the world, they would be poor."

Yet, many would have us to believe that the United States was not founded, defended, and advanced by men of strong Christian faith. Even the general population professed the Christian faith in 1776. At that time, a survey disclosed that 98.6 percent of the people in America claimed to be Christians. Indeed, in 1776 America was a Christian nation and virtually no one would have objected to adding that we were "one nation under God."

But what place did the Christian faith hold in the lives of those who *signed* the Declaration of Independence? Patrick Henry did not sign

66 Kennedy, p. 67.

since he was not a member of congress at the time the Declaration was signed. Nor was George Washington a signer because he was busy at his task of defending his country as Command in Chief of the Continental Army fighting against the British.

However GEORGE WASHINGTON, in his personal prayer book wrote,

> Oh eternal and everlasting God, direct my thoughts, words and work. Wash away my sin in the immaculate blood of the lamb and purge my heart by the Holy Spirit. Daily frame me more and more in the likeness of thy son, Jesus Christ, that living in the fear, I may in thy appointed time obtain the resurrection of the justified unto eternal life. Bless, O Lord, the whole race of mankind and let the world be filled with the knowledge of thy son, Jesus Christ.

Do those words written by the "Father of our country" sound as if they were written by an atheist, humanist, or a non-Christian? Later, in his farewell address on September 19, 1796, Washington reiterated his religious faith and once again stated a significant part of his philosophy of government.

> It is impossible to govern the world without God and the Bible. Of all the dispositions and habits that led to political prosperity, our religion and morality are the indispensable supporters. Let us with caution indulge

> the supposition that morality can be maintained without religion. Reason and experience both forbid us to expect that our national morality can prevail in exclusion of religious principle.

Signers of the Declaration of Independence: Men of Religious Faith

The Revolutionary War was raging. In June, 1776, Patriots had soundly defeated the British Navy at Fort Moultrie, South Carolina. At Philadelphia, in the summer of 1776, delegates of the Continental Congress courageously signed a document declaring independence of the Thirteen Colonies from Great Britain. However, they were not declaring their total independence. They were merely shifting their dependence from Great Britain to their dependence on God.

The opening lines of the Declaration of Independence declare the right to become a separate and equal power among the nations of the earth. They viewed this right as having been granted by “the Law of Nature and Nature’s God”. They wrote that they were “endowed by the Creator with certain unalienable rights.” They went on to include that they were “appealing to the Supreme Judge of the world for the rectitude of their intentions.” They ended the document by asserting that they were declaring themselves independent of the British Crown, but with “a firm reliance on the protection of Divine Providence.”

As an integral part of the wording of the

Declaration of Independence, the members of the Continental Congress affirmed their recognition of God by referring to Him as "Nature's God," "the Creator," "the Supreme Judge of the world," and Divine Providence." That same Congress appointed chaplains for itself and the armed forces, sponsored the publication of a Bible, imposed Christian morality on the armed forces, and granted public lands to promote Christianity among the Indians.[67]

Prior to the American Revolution, the only English Bibles in the colonies were imported either from Europe or England. Publication of the Bible was regulated by the British government, and required a special license. Robert Aitken's Bible was the first known English-language Bible to be printed in America, and also the only Bible to receive *Congressional* approval. Aitken's Bible, sometimes referred to as "The Bible of the Revolution," is one of the rarest books in the world, with few copies still in existence today. On January 21, 1781, Robert Aitken presented a "memorial" [petition] to Congress offering to print "a neat Edition of the Holy Scriptures for the use of schools. After appointing a committee to study the project, Congress acted on September 12,

67 To bring the "good news" to the natives of the New World, the Rev. John Eliot translated Bible into the Massachusetts dialect of the Algonquian language. It was published in Cambridge in 1663 under the title *The Holy Bible Containing the Old Testament and the New Translated into the Indian Language and Ordered to be Printed by the Commissioners of the United Colonies in New England.*

> 1782, by "highly approving of the pious and laudable undertaking of Mr. Aitken." The resolution read as follows: "Whereupon, resolved, that the United States in Congress assembled, highly approve the pious and laudable undertaking of Mr. Aitken, as subservient to the interest of religion, as well as an instance of the progress of arts in this country, and being satisfied from the above report of his care and accuracy in the execution of the work, they recommend this edition of the Bible to the inhabitants of the United States, and hereby authorize him to publish this Recommendation in the manner he shall think proper."[68]

Yet, some still would try to sell Americans on the belief that their founding fathers claimed no place for religion as they framed the new nation. Clearly, the Christian religion was intended to play a significant role in the developing society of the United States of America. Anti-biblical ideology of the Supreme Court and the ACLU were beyond the imagination of our founding fathers.

The Declaration did not say how the country was to be run. That would be the purpose of the Constitution that would not be created until nine years later. What do we know of the place of Christianity in the lives of the fifty-five men who signed the Declaration of Independence, July 4, 1776?

---

68 http://wallbuilders.com/LIBissuesArticles.asp?id=46, 1/30/08

Fifty-two were established members of orthodox established Christian communions. Signers of the Declaration were Catholics, Congregationalists, Quakers, Presbyterians, Episcopalians (Anglicans), and Unitarians (Universalists).

All of the other three believed in the God of Scriptures, that He involved Himself in the affairs of men, and they believed the Bible as the divine truth. Since the sources abound with information about the lives of those men, we will choose only a few whose names tend to be prominent in the minds of even those with only a casual interest in history.

JOHN ADAMS was considered to have one of the best legal minds of his era. He and his wife were dedicated Christians. He viewed the Bible with such esteem that he read five chapters from it each day. On the day the Declaration of Independence was approved by Congress, John Adams wrote to Abigail, "The general principles upon which the fathers achieved independence were the general principles of Christianity. . . I will avow that I believed, and now believe that these general principles of Christianity are as eternal and immutable as the existence and attributes of God." Many historians assume that virtually all who attended the Constitutional Convention had read Adam's book, *A Defense of the Constitutions of Government of the United States*, which he had written with a distinctively Christian view. John Adams served as Governor of New York (1795-1801); vice-president of the American Bible Society

(1816-21) and its president (1821-27)—eleven years of leadership in the American Bible Society. Yet, some would have us to believe that God, as represented in the person of Jesus of Nazareth, was unimportant to the founders of the United States of America.

BENJAMIN FRANKLIN, in a pamphlet *Information to Those Who Would Remove to America* wrote for distribution in Europe,

> . . . serious religion, under its various denominations, is not only tolerated, but respected and practiced. Atheism is unknown there; Infidelity rare and secret; so that persons may live to a great age in that country without having their piety shocked by meeting with an Atheist or an Infidel. And the Divine Being seems to have manifested his approbation of the mutual forbearance and kindness with which the different sects treat each other, by the remarkable prosperity with which he has been pleased to favor the whole country.[69]

We feel safe in assuming that Franklin was better qualified to speak to the religious atmosphere of the North American society of the late eighteenth century than secular theorists more than two centuries later. And we have far more evidence of Franklin's religious interests than that of one mere pamphlet written to persuade Europeans to come to American soil.

69 LaHay, p. 31.

Speaking of his 1749 plan for education for public schools in Pennsylvania, Franklin was recorded to have insisted that schools teach “the excellency of the Christian religion above all others, ancient or modern.” If the ACLU had existed in that day, their leaders would have been foaming at the mouth.

At the Constitutional Convention of 1787, Franklin spoke clearly to his own faith in God and concern for the place of God in the building of the new nation. He stated, “God governs the affairs of man. And if a sparrow cannot fall to the ground without His notice, is it probable that an empire can rise without His aid? We have been assured in the Sacred Writings that except the Lord build the house, they labor in vain who build it. I firmly believe this. I also believe that without His concurring aid, we shall succeed in this political building no better than the builders of Babel.”

In the same year, when Franklin helped found Benjamin Franklin University, it was dedicated as “a nursery of religion and learning, built on Christ, the Cornerstone.” These do not sound like the thoughts of a Deist as some have claimed him to be.

Throughout 1776 the fighting continued. Only weeks after the Declaration of Independence was signed, on August 27, the British defeated the Patriots in the Battle of Long Island, and by September 15, the British were occupying New York City. Courageous colonists remained undeterred. However, the winning of a major battle does not necessitate the winning of a war. The precise date of the war's end is uncertain. Some have said that it simply "petered out." In November of 1782 the British agreed to American Independence and made a preliminary accord with America. In January of 1783 they signed the preliminary peace treaty. On April 14, the Governor of New Jersey issued a Proclamation that ended formal hostilities.

Creators of the Constitution: Men of Religious Faith

Twelve of the thirteen states elected seventy-three men to represent them at the Constitutional Convention that was scheduled to begin meeting on May 14. However, since many arrived late, their meetings in Carpenter's Hall of Philadelphia did not begin until May 25 and continued until September 17, 1787.

Since Rhode Island opposed the union, they failed to elect representatives. Each of the individual states was highly independent and equally highly distrusting of federal governments. Many voices among them all favored the maintenance of thirteen separate sovereign states. At times, some swung close to anarchy. Fortunately, some visionaries could see the possibility of forming a strong federal government without weakening the power of the individual states. The average age of the men was about forty-five years. The youngest man, Dayton, was twenty-six and Franklin, the oldest, was in his eighties. During the convention, men came and went with no more than fifty-five ever present at one time. Although many contributed their thoughts to the deliberations, when time came to vote, only thirty-nine men were present.

The Declaration of Independence, the charter for the new land, had said clearly that the land was to be governed by God's laws. Therefore, all laws of the new nation must be consistent with the laws of God which were to be readily seen in the Scriptures. All representatives were members of established communions, bringing the values fostered by the Christian faith. They consisted of Presbyterians, Catholics, Anglicans/ Episcopalians, Lutherans, Quakers, Methodists, Congregationalists, and Dutch Reformed.

Those who assembled were generally well educated and informed on theories of government that had been influential in the earliest development of the English Parliament and to the Puritan Revolution with its philosophy of democratic government. They were versed in eighteenth century theories of natural law and the natural rights of man. They knew what they wanted and they knew what they did not want. Of course, they were aware of the developing theories of the Enlightenment. However, they were also familiar with the writings of powerful men of influence such as intellectuals John Locke and Charles de Montesque who wrote their philosophies of law from a Biblical world view. John Calvin was such an influence in the minds of the people of that day that one scholar called the finished draft of the Constitutional Convention, "Calvin's Constitution."

The framers of the Constitution knew that the document would have to be ratified by the states, all of which were highly influenced by men of Christian faith and values. Eight states still required that their elected officials must be committed to Christ and members of a church.

When the body of dignitaries assembled the first time, despite the fame many others held in their own right, they unanimously elected George Washington as president. Throughout the convention, James Madison sat at the front, taking copious notes, often working well into the night adding details.

Day after day, men talked. They thought. They debated. By late in July, the summer temperature rose, but tempers flared higher, creating a crisis that endangered dissolution of all efforts to form a Constitution.

BENJAMIN FRANKLIN, the second most respected man in the assembly, gave a speech in which he pled for prayers to be held at the beginning of each day's deliberations. He requested that at the beginning of each day's work, a member of the city's clergy should be present to make petitions before God. Since that time, each day, a member of the clergy has opened both houses of Congress.

By late August, many drafts of recommendations had been rejected. Some had been accepted.

Few historians believe that these men suspected that they were hammering out one of the most important and influential documents ever created in the history of humankind. It would serve as the foundational pattern for the formation of democracies for centuries to come, impacting the lives of uncountable millions.

Knowing that any document that they created would be difficult to get ratified by all the states, some important issues were intentionally bypassed. An incomplete, flawed constitution was better than no constitution at all. Consequently, the Constitution deprived Congress of the right to prohibit the slave trade. Everyone knew that slave-holding states in both the north and south would refuse to ratify a constitution that prohibited the ownership of slaves. That issue would have to wait until the new nation was more firmly bonded. They knew that for the foreseeable future any union would be tenuous at best. A constitution that needed to be improved was better than no constitution at all. By September 17, 1787, the Constitution had been ratified.

The Constitution Needed Amendments

In September 1788, after the necessary three-quarters of the states ratified the Constitution, the existing Congress, under the Articles of Confederation passed a law setting March 4, 1789, as the convening date of the First Congress. Throughout the years, the people felt the need to be protected from a powerful government—even their own. Throughout history, people generally have had more to fear from their own governments than from "foreign" powers. Those present felt secure. They also believed that those who followed them were safe from rule by a government with too much power. The government would not rule their religious life, nor would a religion rule their government.

Much work still needed to be done, but it was time to celebrate. The festivities to celebrate the Constitution's ratification were cheerful and thronged. Benjamin Rush recorded the event. He wrote ecstatically about the religious symbolism he watched.

> "The Clergy formed a very agreeable part of the Procession—They manifested by their attendance, their sense of the connection between religion and good government," Rush said. There were seventeen in all, and they marched in sets, arm in arm. "Pains were taken to connect members of the most dissimilar religious principles together, thereby to show the influence of a free government in promoting Christian charity," Rush said. "The Rabbi of the Jews . . . locked in the arms of two ministers of the gospel was a most delightful sight. There could not have been a more happy emblem contrived of that section of the new constitution which opens all its power and offices alike not only to every sect of Christians, but to worthy men of

> every religion. . . ." Rush added his own musings. "Tis done! We have become a nation." . . . Another observer said, "The Jew joined Christian; the Episcopalian the Presbyterian . . . all walked arm in arm exhibiting a proof of worldly affection, and testify to their approbation of the new constitution."[70]

In obedience to the law passed in the previous September, on March 4, 1789 the First Congress convened.

JAMES MADISON rose early to propose the first of ten amendments that were soon to be added to the Constitution. He wrote in his Federalist Papers (No. 51), "If men were angels, no government would be necessary." He recognized human sinfulness and the need for Godly principles. Historians tell us that Madison earlier had said, "We have staked the whole future of our new nation, not upon the power of government; far from it. We have staked the future of all our political constitutions upon the capacity of each of ourselves to govern ourselves according to the moral principles of the Ten Commandments". (Yet, the Ten Commandments have been removed by the power of the Supreme Court because, "If the posted copies of the Ten Commandments were to have any effect at all, it would be to induce school children to read them. And if they read them, meditated upon them, and perhaps venerated, and observed them, this is

70 Cousins, p. 99.

not a permissible objective.") Such an objective seems to have been admired and not loathed by the founding fathers of the nation who valued not only the Ten Commandments, but the entire Bible and its God. One of the appropriations of that first congress was for the printing of Bibles to be used for the conversion of the Indians.[71]

Some of the results of the distribution of those Bibles became evident when Redbird Smith, a Cherokee stood before the US Senate in c1876. There he protested the white men's violations of the treaties established between the displaced Cherokees from Southern Appalachia to the Oklahoma Territory. He insisted, "I say I will never change before our God, I won't. It extends to Heaven, the great (removal) treaty that has been made with the Government of the United States. Our treaty wherever it extends is respected by the Creator, God." Asserting himself as a Christian brother before them, he was speaking of his God of Christianity and the white man's God of Christianity. A short time later, Willis F. Toby, a full blooded Choctaw Christian, stood before the Senate and declared, "I am still faithful to the great Father of the United States, who made this treaty with the Indians, and I am faithful to that treaty, and the Almighty that rules the world, I trust Him and He will stand as the guardian of my people." Strong Indian Baptist and Methodist churches flourished during this period.[72]

---

71 La Haye, p. 6.

72 Debo, pp. 6-7.

The Christ who had come forth from the tomb continued to change men and women and boys and girls. As people were changed, whole societies continued to change as the Gospel integrated even into the aboriginal societies of the North America.

The Bill of Rights

The amendment to the Constitution that Madison proposed at that first assembly of Congress became the first of the first ten amendments that came to be known as the Bill of Rights. The First Amendment was clear enough for even a school child to understand without "scholarly interpretation" by the Supreme Court. "Congress shall *make no law* respecting an establishment of religion, or prohibiting the free exercise thereof; or abridging the freedom of speech, or of the press, or the right of the people peaceably to assemble, and to petition the government for redress of grievances." What is difficult to understand about the words that prohibit Congress, the state, from establishing a religion? It speaks no words of "separation of church and state."

Eleven years later, when Thomas Jefferson[73] first referred to the "wall of separation" between the church and the state, he was referring to a wall that should keep the government from controlling any

73 Although considered by many as a man void of religious faith, Jefferson once told John Adams that he believed that when we leave "our sorrows and suffering bodies," we would "ascend in essence to an ecstatic meeting with the friends we have loved and lost and whom we shall still love and never lose again" (Meacham, p. 9).

aspect of the church—not to keep religious values out of the government—not for the government to keep religious values from the people. (Recall that the Supreme Court turned this part of the first amendment upside down by their concern that the Ten Commandments might influence the people's conduct.) Although Jefferson may not be viewed by some as a conventional Christian, He was a firm believer in a God who had created the universe. Into Virginia's statute for religious freedom, in 1777 Jefferson penned the opening words, "Whereas Almighty God hath created the mind free. . . ."[74]

On April 30, 1789, in full view of the people, George Washington stepped forth to pick the oath of office of President of the United States and asked for a Bible to be brought to him. On its open pages, he placed his hand while he made his pledge. At the end of the oath, he added the improvised words, "So help me God," and kissed the Bible on which he had sworn it. He then went inside to deliver his inaugural address to Congress. With solemn tones, he spoke:

> It would be peculiarly improper to omit, in this first official act, my fervent supplication to that Almighty Being, who rules over the universe, who presides in the councils of nations, and whose providential aids can supply every human defect, that His benedictions may consecrate to the liberties and happiness of the people of the United

74 Meacham, p. 11.

> States. . . . No people, can be bound to acknowledge and adore the invisible hand which conducts the affairs of men more than the people of the United States. Every step by which they have advanced to the character of an independent nation seems to have been distinguished by some token of providential agency. . . . We ought to be no less persuaded that the propitious smiles of Heaven can never be expected on a nation that disregards the eternal rules of order and right, which Heaven itself has ordained.[75]

Meacham, in his book, *American Gospel* reminds his readers that because of the enduring philosophy of government established by our founding fathers,

> When the president says, 'God bless America, or when we sing 'America, America! God shed His grace on thee,' each American is free to define God in whatever way he chooses. A Christian may summon God the Father; a Jew's Yahweh; a Muslim's Allah; an atheist's; no one, or no thing.[76]

The American society continues to be truly blessed by God upon whom our founders relied.

---

75 Marshal, p. 349.

76 Meacham, p. 23.

But Slavery Continued

Many thousands of Americans have tried to understand how slavery continued without an attempt to end the practice in the United States by the Constitution or the Bill of Rights. The answer is simple, but the reasons are complex.

Some leaders of the various colonies were highly suspicious of a federal government. Each colony had its own set of laws and saw their potential to be an independent, autonomous state when freed from the rule of England. States united under a central government seemed too close to exchanging one bad central government located in Britain for a different bad central government located on their own continent. The creators of the Constitution were trying to write a document that could be ratified by all of the colonies. Many in the colonies wanted to retain the "peculiar institution" of slavery. But our founders were certain that if it was banned by the constitution, the constitution would never be ratified. Therefore, the framers of the constitution were willing to settle for an imperfect constitution, rather than to run the risk of not having the constitution ratified by all of the colonies. They were willing to accept what they could get with the hopes of improving on it later.

Slavery Abolished by Christian Influence

Of course, we know that slavery continued in the United States and in the un-united states until the middle of the nineteenth century after the War for Southern Independence, erroneously called the American Civil War. Civil wars are fought by people who are trying to gain control of a government. Wars of aggression are fought between two or more independent powers—two or more independent governments. The Southern states had legally separated themselves from the United States of America and had formed a separate, independent nation known as the Confederate States of America. They had formed their own government that included a president, a congress, a postal system, a secured currency, and all else that identified themselves as an independent nation.

During the years of the existence of the Confederate States of America, not one slave was ever brought into a southern port by a ship bearing the Confederate flag. All slaves ever brought into the south were bought from northern slave owners. Not for the purpose of freeing the slaves held in both northern and southern states, but for economic causes, the United States of America invaded and eventually conquered the Confederate States of America. That war between the Northern states and the Southern states killed more Americans than the combined numbers that have been killed in all other wars in which Americans have fought throughout the nation's history. Although both Christians and non-Christians died in the war between the United States and the Confederate States of America, Christians of all ethnic backgrounds have opposed slavery and many have sacrificed their lives in their efforts to end the practice.[77]

Back to the Beginning of Slavery

No one seems to know precisely where or when men began to take others as slaves, but we know that it began thousands of years before the birth of Christ. Those who have analyzed history are convinced that they know two reasons how and why slavery began:

Sigmund Freud gained renown for his writings and teachings that grew out of his conviction that the sex drive is the strongest of all human urges. However, others who did not gain the renown of Freud believe that the strongest urge of humanity is the urge to control others, and they can point to countless examples to support their belief. We will not debate that issue at this time. However, we can better understand the urge to force other members of the human race into slavery when we associate this urge with two other controlling phenomenon of "human nature."

(1) Jesus had warned his listeners that the love of money was the root of all evil. Perhaps he was using a hyperbole to emphasize an important truth. Whether money is actually the root of all evil is hardly worth debate. What thinking observer can debate whether the love for money is the greatest root or the second or third greatest root? No one who has investigated the evil phenomenon of slavery can deny that economic gain has always been the highest motive for the buying, selling,

---

77 Kennedy, 1999.

and working of slaves. Cheap labor has always motivated the working of slaves. The "cheap labor" of the slave in the U. S. was cheap only in the eyes of the wealthy. Only about twenty-five percent of the population of the South could afford to buy and maintain a slave. And many who bought them could not afford the financial burden of maintaining them. Where slavery has become unprofitable, the institution of slavery has died, with or without conflict or fanfare.

(2) Throughout thousands of years, until relatively recently, virtually all men have lived by one central belief: might makes right! (Some continue to hold that belief to this day.) The "might makes right" philosophy is also a theological belief that began in earliest antiquity. Everyone knew that the gods were in control of the universe. They capriciously gave gifts to men, and equally capriciously, they took from men. Everything a man had was a gift of the gods—including his cunning and strength. If the gods gave a man the power to take his neighbor's cow, or chickens, or his hut, or his wife and children, he must use the gift the gods had given to him. He must take his neighbors cow or chickens, or his hut, or his wife and children. If he failed to use the gift of power and cunning to take what his neighbor had, he was failing to meet the expectations of the gods. If he failed to meet the expectations of the gods, he would thereby sin against the god. If he sinned against the gods, he could expect the gods to punish him. With this kind of philosophical/

theological belief, men could readily take the neighbor as a slave believing it was the only right or moral thing to do. The gods required it. In one form or another, throughout human history, some form of the "might makes right" philosophy/ theology has prevailed. It most certainly prevailed among those who captured, bought, sold, and worked slaves in the ancient world and in much of the more modern world.

For roughly 500 years, little evidence can be found of slavery in Europe. However, in the seventeenth century, British ships began transporting African slaves to the British West Indies and to the American colonies and Canada. The Portuguese and the Spanish quickly "wanted in on the action" and began shipping slaves to Central and South America. Of course, we are not surprised to know that some erring Christians continued to uphold slavery even into the nineteenth century in North America. However, Christian voices screamed against the practice from the beginning. But few won strong support. Slaves continued to be purchased (often from black slave traders) in Africa and shipped as merchandise to the New World. Despite popular belief, the United States was never the primary holder of African slaves.

Only about 25 percent of the Americans in the South owned slaves before the war between the North and the South. *Many slave owners in both the North and in the South were black. In Charleston, South Carolina, alone, 407 black*

Americans worked black slaves and many black Americans in the North continued to work, buy, and sell slaves until after the end of the war. Of all the Africans taken for slavery during the slave-trading years of the New World, North America received relatively few: about 7 percent. The British and French colonies in the Caribbean and Spanish settlements took the most: 47 percent. Brazil took 41 percent, while the combine numbers received by the Dutch, Danish, and Swedish colonies totaled about 5 percent.[78] Although some members of the clergy strongly supported slavery, by 1830 two-thirds of all leading abolitionists in the U.S. were clergymen—men who preached to their congregations against slavery when to do so placed the speaker's life in peril.

Elijah Lovejoy, a Presbyterian minister of the Gospel became the abolitionist's first martyr when a rioting gang of anti-abolitionists broke into his printing shop and beat him to death. Despite the anti-abolitionist's violent methods, once the spark had ignited outrage against slavery, Christian opponents to slavery would not be silenced. Some courageous clergymen, convinced that their faith condemned slavery, were imprisoned. Others lost their places of ministry. Influential parishioners could not tolerate the claims of their clergy that slavery was a moral evil and that Christians were morally obligated to oppose slavery. Those who study the history of the period seem to be in accord with the opinion that the influence of

78 Schmidt, p. 278.

Christianity was the primary driving force that ended slavery on the North American continent. However, slavery did not end when it ended in North America.

> Many do not know that the tragedy of slavery continued in a number of countries for more than a hundred years after it was outlawed in the United States in 1865. Ethiopia had slavery until 1942, Saudi Arabia until 1962, Peru until 1964, and India until 1976. Moreover, it still exists to this day in Sudan, Africa's largest country.[79]

As Christians continue to go into various parts of the world, they slowly integrate into the society where they eventually influence change. Where unrighteousness has flourished in the world, followers of Christ have struggled to eliminate it. Even cannibalism, having been practiced for many centuries among various peoples of the earth, has disappeared when Christianity has arrived.

---

79 Schmidt, p. 273.

Chapter 5

Christianity Continued to Change the Whole World

It is not only social change that Christianity has repeatedly influenced. Christianity in various societies has repeatedly influenced the perception of the nature of the world around them. Prior to Christ's influence on the world, beliefs in capricious gods distorted humankind's view of the world, thereby prohibiting progress.

Christianity Opened Doors to Scientific Investigation

The late sixteenth and early seventeenth century experienced a monumental influence by Christian thinkers of the era. Throughout history events we attribute to "natural phenomenon" and even humans themselves were believed to be controlled by the stars, by spirits (both, good and evil), or by the seemingly capricious hand of gods, or of God. However, Thomas Jefferson, supported by other men of science, believed in the power of rational observation, dismissing much of that which has been called supernatural as superstition.

Religionists were also beginning to agree that humans are free moral agents whom God has permitted to make independent decisions. Not only is God not in absolute control of the will of man, He is not in absolute manipulative control of every event.

(If a man drops a pencil, God has not knocked it from his hand, nor is God punishing people by giving them a cold when they have picked up a virus they could have avoided if they had washed their contaminated hands. Although some view the Great Tsunami of December 26, 2004 that killed hundreds of thousands to have been "an act of God," others accept the event as a "cause and effect" event that resulted from a great earth quake at the bottom of the Indian Ocean that resulted from an upheaval in the molten core of the earth. The "act of God" group will then counter that God initiated the molten upheaval. Who is knowledgeable enough of God to determine when He does or does not act?"

It is no mere quirk in history that the greatest advancements in science developed first in those societies most influenced by Christian perceptions of the nature of God and His world. Christianity, with its Judaic roots, accepts one God who is highly rational in all that He does. Since God created humankind in His own image, humans as rational beings could or should use their rational ability to study–to better understand the world in which God had placed them. God created an orderly world of cause and effect that is governed by laws of physics. They are dependable. They do not change. Once discovered, the laws of electromagnetism, gravity, momentum, thermodynamics, planetary motion, and a host of others established the orderliness and predictability of events.

By early in the thirteenth century, a Franciscan bishop and the first chancellor of Oxford University proposed the inductive, experimental method for acquiring knowledge of their world. One of his students, Roger Bacon, a devout student also of the Scriptures argued that knowledge needed to be derived and verified inductively. Bacon insisted that God had given two important books to humankind; the Bible and His created world. He believed that man could never search too deeply into either. Experimentation was not only possible, but could be replicated with predictable results. His book, Instauration Magna (the Great Design) set forth a pattern for post-graduate education and research around it.[80]

Men of Christian faith had crashed the door open to scientific investigation such as humans had never before dreamed possible. Other Christians quickly walked through that door. Every school-child knows the names of Galileo, Isaac Newton, Leonardo de Vinci, Copernicus,

80 Aitken, et. al. p. 59.

Kepler, Ohm, Ampere, Volta, Faraday, Kelvin, Boyle, Lavoisier, Priestley, Pasteur, and George Washington Carver. All were devoted followers of Jesus Christ.

However, we must admit that Christ's church did not always support the early scientists and often fought against them—especially opposing the dissection of cadavers.

> . . . in the fifteenth and sixteenth centuries, the church's theologians and natural philosophers were so firmly wedded to Aristotle's deductive philosophy and Galen's writings that they saw the new methodology of science, such as dissecting human bodies, as wrong. Thus, it was not biblical or Christian doctrine that prompted opposition to dissection of cadavers, or to other aspects of science, but rather it was the pagan Greek theories that a few theologians within the church saw as the final word.[81]

Antony Van Leeuwenhoek of Deft, Holland, became a master of the craft of grinding lenses with which he is known to have made more than 400 microscopes. In 1673, he began writing letters to the newly-formed Royal Society of London, describing bacteria that he had been viewing with his microscopes. Roughly two centuries would pass before Joseph Lister of Glasgow, Scotland, learned by experimentation

---

81 Schmidt, p. 237.

that a chemical, carbolic acid, when sprayed on surgical instruments and bandages, infections dramatically stopped bacterial spread. Lister continued his experiments for two years, and in 1867 made public that carbolic acid was an *antiseptic*, i.e. it prevented the wounds he had treated from going septic.

Patients with wounds had been dying, not because God does what He wants to do when He wants to do. They were being killed by bacteria—the peculiar little creatures about which Van Leeuwenhoek had written. These men were the products of a society influenced by Christians who were increasingly convinced that we live in God's orderly world of cause and effect. Under the Christian banner, more direct social changes were taking place during the nineteenth century.

Christianity Responsible for Child Labor Laws

Until that time, those who were not Christians had continued to use and abuse children in places of work. Only by the efforts of Christians represented by Lord Shaftesbury of the English Parliament were child labor laws passed in Britain, thereby setting precedents for similar laws that were brought into force in other lands. Countries in which Christianity has had little impact, to this day, force children into dreaded forced labor tasks in fields and factories. Often slower than desired, other changes have been brought about by the impact of Christianity on societies. When sanctions are declared against nations that violate human rights, they are enforced largely on the basis Christian values.

Christianity Continued to Elevate the Value of Women

William Carey, a Christian missionary in India, and others under the influence of Christian morality brought about the virtual end of *suttee,* the Hindu practice in which women voluntarily incinerated themselves or were forcibly burned alive on the funeral pyre of their deceased husbands. When religion and society are thoroughly integrated, change is often slow. Although the legislation against *suttee* was passed in 1929, reports as recent as 2006 tell us that the practice occasionally emerges.

Jesus did not want to burn widows. He wanted the society in which they lived to protect and care for them. Across the centuries, the Gospel of Jesus the Christ has quickened the conscience of individuals and spread its influence into entire societies. The beginning of Jesus' ministry in remote little Galilee, marks the turning point in the history of women around the world. Alvin Schmidt, quoting George Morrison said, "Whatever else our Lord did, He immeasurably exalted women." He went on to add:

> Yet neither Christ nor the early Christians preached an outright revolution. Rather it was His example that His followers reflected in their relationships with women raising

> their dignity, freedom, and rights to a level previously unknown in any culture. One needs only to remember how badly women were treated by the Greeks, Romans, Hindus, and the Chinese and by many other societies where paganism prevailed. Before Christianity arrived century upon century had brought little or no freedom or dignity in any pagan culture. In short, where else do women have more freedom, opportunity, and human worth than in countries that have been highly influenced by the Christian ethic?[82]

While we are on the subject of significant social changes brought about by Christians in our more modern era, we can see a highly significant social change influenced by Christians in the Philippines.

In the middle 1950s, I was stationed on Okinawa. We were ordered to fly our B-29 Bomber into Clark Air Force Base on the Philippine island of Luzon. Of course, our eleven-man crew attended an intelligence briefing before the flight. Near the end of the briefing, the officer in charge warned us that when we "coasted in" to Luzon, under no circumstance were we to fly over the northeastern coast of the island. We were to fly only over the northeastern coast as we flew southward toward Clark AFB. Our navigator was making notes.

Having recently graduated from the Air Force

82 Schmidt, p 122.

Pilot Training School and commissioned as a Second Lieutenant, my curiosity was aroused. My hand went up. “Sir! You have emphasized that we should not fly over the northeastern sector of Luzon. Is it in order for me to ask you, why?” He responded, “Lieutenant, it’s obvious that you are not yet experienced in flying in this part of the world. During WW II the Japanese boasted that they controlled the Philippine Islands, but nobody in history has ever controlled the headhunters and cannibals of northeastern Luzon. Nobody rules them today. If you were to experience engine trouble and had to make a forced landing, you and your entire crew would be eaten by the cannibals.” I am sure that my eyes widened, and my jaw dropped. He had made his case. I did not know that headhunting and cannibalism still existed on our planet in the mid 1950s. And they were only a few hundred miles across the South China Sea from me.

A few years later, the northeastern sector of Luzon was forcefully taken under the rule of the Philippine government. Efforts to change their practices by education and persuasion had little effect. In 1966 Ferdinand Marcos was elected as the first President of the Philippine Islands. The atmosphere was conditioned for change. Under the strong, persistent, pressure by Christians of the Philippine Islands, lawmakers passed laws that prohibited cannibalism. The Philippine government had the power of the Philippine military force to enforce it. A missionary, home on furlough, recently told me that no evidence exists that cannibalism continues in the Philippines. Centuries of cultural behavior was ended by education and by laws supported by power, both strongly influenced by Christianity.

Although knowledge of right does not always result in right behavior, without knowledge of right, evil tends to roam unleashed. Again we are indebted to Charlemagne who so strongly promoted the passing on of knowledge—education for all people.

As dominos knock down dominos, the influence of Charlemagne on the educational system of Europe continued on that continent and on to the North American Continent and on around the world. The sciences perhaps have brought some of the most notable changes. Some have been for the benefit of humankind, but unfortunately some have been terribly destructive.

By the beginning of the twenty-first century the sciences have mushroomed and the knowledge gained from them is doubling at least every twenty years. Various sources give varying estimates. Some tell us that knowledge is doubling every seven years, and some even suggest fourteen months. Perhaps no one really knows how rapidly knowledge is growing. Even if we doubt all of the estimates, we concede that the growth is beyond most people's ability to comprehend.

With the send-off of our founding fathers, the nation's society flourished for almost a hundred-fifty year. Isaac Newton's law of physics, the "first law of motion," often called the Law of Momentum, states that a "body at rest continues at rest and a body in motion continues in uniform motion in a straight line unless acted upon by an external force." The Law of Motion has an application in the realm of human emotions, economics, and many others, including in the realm of society in general. With notable exceptions, the North American society continued to uphold its religious-moral values for roughly one hundred fifty years.

But Evil Coexists with Good

One "notable exception" developed soon after the close of the War for Southern Independence, commonly called the American Civil War. Without attempting to unravel the confusing origins of the Ku Klux Klan (KKK), we cannot avoid reference to their terrorist activities that were widely sanctioned by the church. When religion does not adequately influence the society, the society will influence the religion. The society was so permeated with a violent spirit, that violent spirit became integrated into its church. With a membership that included so many men of the church, the KKK has been regarded by some historians as a church—a Christian denomination. However, terrorist activities have never been tolerated by true followers of Jesus Christ. Once again, Christian influences have even pricked the conscience of evil men. Always with the possibility of gaining strength again, early in the twenty-first century, the KKK is impotent. Through the first half of the twentieth century, the North American society continued on its uncertain course.

Then that society began to break apart and plummet toward total destruction reminiscent of the ill-fated shuttle, Challenger, that exploded seventy-three seconds after liftoff on January 26, 1986. If the current generation fails to halt the rapidly increasing moral decay, future generations are in danger of existing in a corner of something close to Hell here on earth.

Chapter 6

Christianity Sounds a Disaster Alert!

Modern aircraft carry devices that warn of thunderstorms in their path of flight. (Even fifty years ago, my radar operator guided me through a cluster of thunderstorms while flying a B-29 Superfortress at night over the Gulf of Mexico.) The daily newspapers and the daily television newscasts in every city of North America carry warnings of disaster ahead for the entire society. When they are viewed individually, they may seem innocuous; however, when viewed as a whole, they point to disaster.

Many alive today can remember when few people locked the doors on their homes when they were away for a few hours. Virtually every school boy carried a pocket knife. No parent worried about his or he child being shot in school. (When my brother was in school, he sometimes went rabbit hunting before going to school. At school, he simply propped his .22 rifle outside the classroom door until he carried it home at the end of the day.) Children who lived in rural areas disappeared to play in the fields and woodlands until they reappeared for lunch, only to disappear for the remainder of the day without parents worrying about their children being molested by predators.

Drugs, primarily heroin, some opium and cocaine, were limited to the back streets of New York, Chicago, Los Angeles, and the "opium dens" of far away places in the Orient.[83] Few people were afraid to pick up hitch-hikers. (During a period of my late youth and young adulthood, I hitch-hiked roughly 14,000 miles without once feeling threatened.) Visitors routinely gave New Testaments to children in public schools across the U.S. No one considered the need to escort children to school restrooms. Newspapers occasionally carried a story of a truck load of liquor having been hijacked, but no one had ever heard of a carjacking. Indeed, carjacking is a relatively new word in the North American vocabulary.

In 1942, four percent of all births in the U.S. were without the benefits of marriage, but births to unwed mothers began to rise steadily reaching more than thirty-three percent in the year 2006. The United States has the highest rates of teen pregnancy and births in the western industrialized

83 While I served as an Air Force pilot immediately following the Korean War, I satisfied youthful curiosity by visiting a legal opium den in Bangkok, Thailand. I have been told that they are no longer lawful and have been closed.

world. Teen pregnancy costs the United States at least $9 billion annually. Thirty-one percent of young women become pregnant at least once before they reach the age of 20—about 750,000 a year. Eight in ten of these pregnancies are unintended and 81 percent are to unmarried teens. However, teachers in public schools supported by taxes are forbidden to teach abstinence from sexual intercourse until marriage because abstinence is a teaching from a religion. (What moral value is not a teaching from some religion?)

> According to Cornell law professor Gary Simson,[84] sex education courses that teach abstinence until marriage are unconstitutional because they violate the Establishment Clause of the First Amendment. Simson says recommending sexual abstinence to teenagers is wrong because it 'teaches that this one belief is the only proper one.'[85]

Child molesters are known to slither through the streets of virtually every community. Police must patrol the halls of our schools and even have to ride our school busses. Writers for the television and theater industries, the products of the liberal, godless, amoral educational system, continue to crank out an endless stream of material that glorifies extra-marital sex relationships, perversions, and violence. (A

---

84 Related to the comic strip characters?

85 Coulter, p.12.

counselee once said to me that she had grown up with no clear pattern of behavior evident in the people around her. Therefore, she simply watched television and lived her life as those people do. And she could not understand why her life with all her relationships was in such chaos.)

Children walk through metal detectors to get into school and policemen walk their halls to protect them. Yet, they are not even safe in their own yards or behind closed doors of their homes. In my home town, two children have been gunned down in "drive-by shootings" in recent months—one played in her yard and the other sat inside watching television. But the Supreme Court denies the display of the Ten Commandments in schools because they are from the Judeo-Christian religions and the children might be influenced by them. They might take seriously the admonition, "Do Not Murder!" HEAVEN FORBID! Their little psyches might be influenced for life! They might never gun down a classmate or shoot a child playing in her own front yard.[86]

During the first four years of the War in Iraq, roughly 3,000 Americans were killed by warring factions of Muslims in Iraq, and thousands of people repeatedly marched on Washington and other major population centers to protest the war. During the same period, roughly 5,200,000 American babies were executed by Americans in the name of "freedom of choice," "family

86 Another coincident: While proofreading these paragraphs before submitting this manuscript to a publisher, in the background I heard a news report of a teen-age boy who entered a classroom and shot three fellow students.

planning," and "women's right to control their own bodies." Only an occasional voice cries in the ugly wilderness of tiny bodies that have had their brains sucked out in "partial birth" abortions.

And where are the marchers, their bullhorns, and their placards protesting the killing of more than 170,500 Americans by their own drunken countrymen on American highways during that same four year period in which 3000 Americans died in Iraq? They are conspicuously absent, hiding silently behind a thin veil of hypocrisy. They major on the lesser evil and leave the greater evil without objection. It is easier to arouse emotions against military activity than to arouse emotions against socially accepted drunkenness. The concern here is not for the actions of the protestors, but for American silence—the lack of response to the slaughter tolerated on our highways. When enough voices demand action by lawmakers, laws of the land will require confiscation of every automobile driven by drinking drivers after their first DUI conviction. We can only speculate on how historians will look back in wonder at the moral inconsistencies in the North American society of the late twentieth and early twenty-first century. The Christian Law of Love (*agapé*) as taught by Jesus and recorded in the Bible demands reform.

In the early years of U.S. history, one of the most important purposes for education was to teach Biblical truth. Today, in lieu of Biblical truth, "the government schools teach an amalgam of liberalism, feminism, Darwinism, and the Playboy philosophy."[87] And except for a few voices crying in the frightening wilderness, the sound of silence is deafening.

Millions of men and women have taken courses for self-defense, and more carry handgun permits issued for self-defense and for the defense of their family. Still more carry pepper maze when on the street or when locked in the steel cages of their own automobile, feeling safe neither at night nor during daylight hours. Need we speak of the numerous scandals among both, officials of government and officials of corporate giants? At the writing of these words, men are being tried in federal court for a host of criminal behaviors. Few intelligent adults would challenge as fact that in North America the last fifty years have experienced a drastic decline in its moral climate. Within the last week, I listened while a forty year old woman lamented the moral decline she had witnessed in her brief span of life.

When the lack of morality has grown so rapidly that even forty year olds have watched it, that fact alone should serve as an alarm–a "wake-up call" across the land. All of nature abhors a vacuum. Where it exists, something is trying to fill the void. Early, in the twenty-first century, one threat—perhaps the strongest threat stands poised to fill the void as it already has done in England. Melanie Phillips, convinced by the evidence, has written of a series of events that have thrown the

87 Coulter, p. 11.

doors open to Muslims of every spirit. Slowly, and deliberately they have taken the land that once fostered the growth of the Puritans and turned it into an international prep-school for terrorism.

> Britain has become a largely post-Christian society, where traditional morality has been systematically undermined and replaced by an "anything goes" culture in which autonomous decisions about codes of behavior have become unchallengeable rights. With everyone's lifestyle now said to be of equal value, the very idea of moral norms is frowned upon as a vehicle for discrimination and prejudice. Judaism and Christianity, the creeds that formed the bedrock of Western civilization, have been pushed aside and their place filled by a plethora of paranormal activities and cults. . . .[88]

In her book, *Londonistan,* Phillips later says that the Muslims are as "incredulous as they are disgusted" at the rout of moral values that has taken place. She adds that, "in Britain, this decadence not only fuels the rage of Muslims at the moral squalor that so affronts them, it also provides an opportunity to fill with Islamic perspective the space that has been vacated by the collapse of the Judeo-Christian moral authority". Under the ruse of multiculturalism and promoting 'diversity,' local authorities and governmental

88 Phillips, p. xx.

bodies are systematically bullying the expression of Christian values out of existence. As authorities have done in Britain, similar authorities are doing in North America. In both realms, "political correctness" and the fear of offending overrides all else.

In 2006, Muslims in Britain numbered roughly 1.6 million among the overall population of 60 million. However, "more people go to the mosque each week than now attend an Anglican Church.

With a moral climate too similar to that in the United States, London has become home to the largest collection of Islamic activists since the terrorist training lines that were established in Afghanistan. Indeed, it was in Britain that the global Islamic terrorist group, *al-Queda* was formed. The citizens suddenly awakened to the realization that their own British-born, intelligent, well-educated, and affluent young adults were willing and ready to turn themselves into human bombs for the destruction of life aboard buses, airplanes, and other highly visible collections of people.

Throughout history, the morals of a people have been guided by their religion. (The Alabama Supreme Court has declared Secular Humanism a religion.) When secular humanists, Muslims, atheists, and a host of other religious influences have been permitted to take over the control of the writing and publishing of American history school books, totally eliminating the influences of Christianity in the lives of the founding fathers;

when secular humanists, Muslims, atheists, and a host of other religious influences have been permitted to take over the entire public and much of the private educational systems; when liberal atheistic and secular humanists of the U.S. Supreme court have been permitted to reinterpret the Constitution of the United States,[89] we should expect to see the precise decline of obedience to Christian values across the country that we are seeing. The moral climate of the land is killing its people.

---

89 The best synopsis of the issues at hand that I have read are detailed in Tim LaHay's book *Faith of our Founding Fathers* listed in the Bibliography at the end of this work. I wish that every concerned American would read it,

Chapter 7

Even the Modern Church Is Dying

When religion inadequately changes a society, the society changes the religion. Despite the best efforts of thousands of loyal and concerned church leaders, the church across America is in trouble. It is being influenced by the society in which it exists.

For many years, the secular world has looked at the church of North America with disgust. "It's dead," some have said. Others have said, "It's irrelevant. It's only a club of the self-righteous." Others charge that, "It makes no real improvement in the world or even in individual lives," Most simply ignore it. We of the church have rarely paused long enough to examine the indictments for some element of truth.

When words of criticism have reached the muffled ears of the modern church we have self-righteously failed to show enough respect for the critics to give them credibility. Like a fat giant, the church has barely roused from its slumber, grunted, "Not so," rolled over and sunk back into a state of unconsciousness. If the church has stirred at all, it has rubbed its sleepy eyes and pointed to some of its true saints and many faithful servants without looking at the larger body of those who profess its faith. If you think I exaggerate, be patient.

When I speak of the modern church, my use of the word "modern" has no direct reference to the "modern" and "post-modern" schools of philosophical thought. When I speak of the sin of the "modern" church, I speak of the church of today—the church at large of the early twenty-first century.

I've long held a fascination with the message of Jesus. For the harlot, the traitorous tax collectors, and "sinners," he showed compassion, tenderness, and patience. But for the Pharisees and Sadducees—the leaders of the organized religion of His beloved Jewish people, Jesus made blistering attacks. He called them snakes and whitewashed tombs. When He pointed to their sin, they pointed to their tithes and sacrifices. We can only wonder what He wants to say to those of us who make up the modern church.

If someone points out a weakness in the church, we are tempted to point to some strength, without looking for possible truth in the critical statement. In the marriage counseling office, if a woman points to the fact that her husband never takes her out for fun time together, he angrily points out her error: "You forget! I recently took you out to dinner and a movie. We saw 'Titanic.'" She responds, "Yes, we did. That was more than two years ago." First century Jews did not want to hear of their sin, spouses do not want to hear of their sin, and the church has pointed to its many successes, while refusing to look at the sin within it.

A story has been told that a reporter once said to President Abraham Lincoln, "Mr. President, General Harrison has called you a fool. What is your response to General Harrison? Mr. Lincoln is said to have slowly stroked his beard and replied, "I respect General Harrison's opinion. I guess I'd better examine his statement and see what truth I can find in it." Perhaps we of the modern church should listen more closely to our critics. It has been said that the only people who tell us the truth about ourselves are those who either despise us most or those who love us the most.

Since I am going to have much to say about the definitions of words in the pages ahead, let's begin with some definitions here. Already, I have made references to the "church." Since I have done little travel outside the United States in recent years, I can speak only of that which I see in the United States. Therefore, when I speak of the church, I refer to the church in the United States of America. I'll let others make their observations about the church in other countries.

Unfortunately when someone speaks of the

Church, they often are assumed to refer to the Roman Catholic Church. Although I include the Roman Catholic Church in my concern, throughout this chapter, when I speak of the church, I refer to **all** organized Christianity in the United States. I am fully aware that in the New Testament, with few exceptions, the word church relates to a local body of believers. I refer to both, the thousands of local churches and the larger body that makes up Christ's Universal Church. And when I speak of the "sin" of the modern church, I use the classical Hebrew definition of sin as borrowed from the language of the archer who shoots at a target and "misses the mark." It can also mean to err or wander from the path of uprightness, or to violate God's law.

Many years ago, while studying the New Testament, I became aware that everything Jesus asked His followers to do was ultimately for the benefit of the follower and/or the follower's neighbor. Later, I realized that the Ten Commandments that God gave the Israelites through Moses on Mt. Sinai all were given for the benefit of His people. Even later, I realized that because He loves humankind, everything that God has ever asked of His people has always been for the benefit of His people. If all behaviors directed by God are for the benefit of human beings, we see a profound principle. Sin may be understood as any behavior or attitude that harms any human being or fails to promote the best interests of any human being. Such behavior is in violation of the established will of God, an offense against the part of His nature that loves and demands love. In brief, I sin when I do anything that harms any human being—even the one who lives in my skin. Still further, I sin any time I fail to do that which promotes the true welfare of any human being—even the one who lives in my skin.

Both the Old Testament and the New Testament declare that, "the wages of sin is death." And the sins of the modern church are truly deadly. The church's influence on its own members is dying. Its respect by the world is dying. And its impact for positive change on America's society is dying. At least one denomination is seeing its negative influence spilling over into its foreign mission work. Up to 80% of their mission converts are lost within *two months* of their baptism and as many as 30-40% of their new converts in some missions never return to worship in a church after baptism. Denominational leaders are watching the steady decline in attendance and membership across the U.S. Some denominations that boast the greatest numbers cannot find fifty percent of their members. They literally do not know where they are.

The church in America may truly die. However, from the days of Noah, God has always managed to save a remnant of people who remained faithful. While the more theologically liberal churches watch a decline, the most theologically <u>conservative</u> watch a slow, but steady growth.[90] Is

90 To read the reports by denominational headquarters, go to the World Wide Web and sign on to Google.com. Type "Denominational Membership Statistics."

the laity trying to tell the clergy something?

If the church dies in America, God will save a remnant, but America's place as a strong "Christian nation" may be too near death to survive. Many already are referring to post-Christian America. The greatest hope for survival and fresh leadership of the Christian faith may lie in South Korea! Contrary to the thought of many minds, it could come from Russia or China. In the meantime, if the church is to be saved in America, we may need to place it in an Intensive Care Unit. Perhaps the pages ahead will stimulate efforts for treatment.

As a young man, beginning to study for the ministry, I had a pivotal moment in my thought. After having piloted heavy bombers, B-29s during the Korean War, I had enrolled at Furman University to prepare for the gospel ministry. Needing a place to "practice preaching," I had joined a group of other young men who preached each week at the local city jail. In the mid 1950s, we had life term prisoners farmed out from the South Carolina State Penitentiary to local city jails. From week to week, in the City Jail of Greenville, S.C., I found among those criminals—among those from whom society needed protection—among those men who did not need to be persuaded that they had done wrong—I found men I liked. I found little sham and pretense. I found men who accepted Christ's message that called for repentance and offered the grace of forgiveness and regeneration. Even so, it also was there that I had an experience that screamed, "Something's wrong!"

Among those life-term prisoners in the city jail were also drunks from off the street who were in for overnight lock-up. (We were not permitted to mingle with them. We were separated by bars.) One evening, a drunk stumbled to the bars, and held on to keep from falling. In the midst of my sermon, he yelled, "I don't need to hear what you've got to say, preacher! I was saved back there some thirty-five years ago and, praise God, once saved—always saved!" As he yelled the last words, he slid down the bars, lost consciousness, and lay in a heap at my feet. I stood in surprised silence.

Somewhere inside, a voice screamed, "Something's wrong here! He believes he's 'saved' but from all appearances, he's as lost as a man in the middle of the Pacific Ocean in a canoe without a paddle or a compass. He doesn't have to wait for Hell. He's already in a corner of it and doesn't even know it!" Here at my feet lay a man who had walked the aisle of some church in years gone by. He had filled out a form, had spoken the right words to the pastor, but had walked out of the church unrepentant and unregenerate, having tried to accept Christ his Savior without having accepted Christ as Lord of his life.

Those of us who are members of a church tend to be proud of our church. We form friendships and think of one another as brothers and sisters in the faith. Occasionally, we learn of fellow members who are consistently living entirely contrary to the teachings of Jesus Christ, our Lord. We feel disappointed, even saddened. We may even wonder, "How can *Christians* act like that?" If we secretly suspect they may not truly be Christians, we feel guilty, telling ourselves that we should not make such judgments; we should leave judgment to God. We may even quote the words of Jesus to ourselves, "Judge not, and ye shall not be judged. . ." (Lk. 6:37). We will leave each person to hear the judgment of God as God chooses to speak. Judgment may be harsh for those who "profess that they know God; but in works they deny him" (Titus1:16). Speaking of judgment, Jesus warned that He would declare, "Depart from me, ye that work iniquity."

While we try not to judge, and may feel guilty when we find ourselves doing so, we may remember other words of Jesus, "By their fruits ye shall know them" (Matt. 7:20). Although God has not called us to serve as "fruit inspectors," some "fruit" is so good and some is so bad that its quality is obvious to people both inside and outside the church. When I worked in a peach packing shed in South Carolina during my youth, some fruit was so rotten that its condition was obvious to anyone who glanced at it. Most was good and sound.

Any honest assessment must recognize some of the most honorable, honest, loving, caring, and noble souls on earth make up a large segment of the church. However, at the same time any honest assessment must recognize that some of the most dishonorable, dishonest, unloving, uncaring, and ignoble souls on earth also make up a component of the church. Both those who are outside the church and those within the church observe the evidence that declares, "Something's wrong."

Even a superficial reading of the New Testament makes clear that Christians are a different people—so different that to become Christians, they were required to be born anew–from above to gain membership in the Kingdom of God. Lives of Christ's early followers were so changed—so patterned—so modeled after their Lord that they were accused of turning the world upside down (Acts 17:6).

What, then, are some of the sins that are working to kill the church?

Emergence of Angry, Hostile Liberalism

For more than half a century, organized Christianity has been under attack by a system of liberal teachings that earlier Christians would have called "heresy." In mid 2007, a reporter on a major national news network told of a well known clergyman who had said that, "since Christians and Muslims worship the same God, for the sake of harmony, Christians should begin to call the God and Father of Jesus Christ, 'Allah.'" We do not question as fact that the Aramaic language was common to the people of Jesus' Palestine, and the common word for God in the Aramaic language was "Allah." However, God as worshipped and revealed in Jesus is a far different God than the god worshipped by Muhammad.[91]

Because the Christian religion has failed to adequately influence the society, the society is influencing the religion. Weak Christians have permitted or even encouraged a large percent of their clergy in the mainline churches to espouse liberal theology and to undermine confidence in the God of the Bible and of the recreative power of His Son, Jesus Christ. Too many have repeated the Apostles' Creed as a congregation and have then listened, tolerated, and sometimes required the clergy to slowly and methodically deny every phrase of it! I have heard it! For those not familiar with the Apostles' Creed, I quote it; with teachings I have heard or read from liberal clergymen italicized in parentheses:

1. I believe in God the Father, Almighty, Creator of heaven and earth:
   (God did not really create the world. It and all else has evolved over millions of years without assistance by God.)
2. And in Jesus Christ, His only begotten Son, our Lord:
   (Jesus was an unusually brilliant teacher, but he was only the son born of Joseph and Mary, or just as likely, he was the son of Mary and a Roman soldier).
3. Who was conceived by the Holy Ghost, born of the Virgin Mary:
   (*It is impossible for a virgin to give birth.*)

---

91 This statement is supported by numerous biographical works on Muhammad with Ibn Ishaq's, *The Life of Muhammad*, as representative of those I have read.

4. Suffered under Pontius Pilate; was crucified, dead and buried: He descended into hell:
   (*Hell is not really a place or state. It is the grave.*)
5. The third day he rose again from the dead:
   (*The so-called witnesses of Jesus' life after a so-called resurrection were lying or were hallucinating.*)
6. He ascended into heaven, and sits at the right hand of God the Father Almighty:
   (*His dust is still somewhere in Palestine, since there is no resurrection from the dead by anyone.*)
7. From thence he shall come to judge the quick and the dead:
   (*Since he remains dead, he cannot come back to do anything.*)
8. I believe in the Holy Ghost:
9. I believe in the holy catholic (universal) church: the communion of saints:
   (*The church is only an organization for the get-together of Christians.*)
10. The forgiveness of sins:
    (*Of course we are forgiven. God holds nothing against any person.*)
11. The resurrection of the body:
    (*The idea of a resurrection of the dead is only a fantasy wish begun by people even before the days of the ancient Egyptians.*)
12. And the life everlasting.
    (*Again, the idea of anyone living forever is*

a carryover from the days of the ancient Egyptian pharaohs.)

Heresies such as these italicized in parentheses have been fostered by liberal seminaries and writers also teaching that virtually everything the Bible quotes Jesus as having said are highly doubtful if not totally inaccurate.[92]

Coincidental to the writing of the previous paragraphs on this subject, my phone rang. When I told the woman of the subject about which I am writing, she said, "They taught me in college that the best way to destroy a society is to first destroy its religion." They taught her correctly. Until we are able to rebuild the Christian religion in this country (and the UK) we can expect the current degradation of our society to continue.

Not only have liberal religionists essentially abandoned the foundations of Christianity, they have developed a hostile, militant assault on those with whom they disagree. They can no longer agreeably disagree. They display an attitude that conveys, "You are an ignorant fool if you disagree with me. You are so far beneath me that I do not want you around me or those in my sphere of life." I know of more than one institutional minister who was dismissed because of such an attitude. One was dismissed when the administrator learned that his institutional staff minister was a graduate of XYZ seminary known for its strongly conservative stance.

---

92 Funk, R.W., et. al.

Failure to Submit to the Rule of Jesus the Christ

The modern church has failed to accept and to promote one of the most elementary tenets of the Christian faith: Jesus is the Christ; the Messiah; the King. In daily conversation we may speak of Jesus, or of Christ, or we may speak of Jesus Christ. In a culture that has thoroughly integrated the language of the Christian faith, we use all three ways of referring to Jesus as if all three were His name. Indeed, many people who have been members of the church for many years assume that Jesus Christ is His first and last name.

In the first century Mediterranean world, few men carried a sir name. A male was often identified by his home town. Jesus was often called "Jesus of Nazareth" and we the Bible speaks of "Joseph of Arimathaea." However, more often men were referred to as the son of his father or the son of the man known for his craft. Therefore, in Nazareth, the small, insignificant village of eighty to one hundred houses and three hundred to five hundred residents, Jesus probably would have been known as Jesus Bar (son of) Joseph. Or He might have been known as *Yeshua Bar Tekton,* (Jesus son of a Carpenter). Christ was the identifying title of His adult role as God's Savior-King whose coming had been foretold for many hundreds of years.

For more than a thousand years before Jesus' birth, the Jews had used the title "King" and

"Anointed One" *completely interchangeably.* A newly proclaimed king might have enjoyed having someone place a crown or golden war-helmet on his head. He also might have enjoyed receiving a costly breastplate with magnificent jewels and mounds of gold and silver, but these were only signs of his having been named as the people's king. Kingship was created only by *the olive oil that was poured over his head* from a vile. His head was *anointed.* Saul had been the first man anointed as king over those loosely knit tribes who later became known as Jews.

The Hebrew word for "to anoint" was *mashah,* and "the Anointed One" was called the *Mashih.* When that word was translated into the European languages fifteen hundred years after Jesus' birth, it became "Messiah." Unlike the Old Testament, which was written in the Hebrew language, the New Testament was written in Greek. The word "Messiah" when translated into Greek becomes, "Christ." In the briefest statement, the word "Messiah" and the word "Christ" mean precisely the same. They both refer to God's anointed King over His people.

In modern North America, most of us are too far removed from kings and queens to comprehend their role in ancient history. In the first century, everyone in the civilized world, and many in the not so civilized world, understood precisely the power and role of a king.

A king was the absolute ruler over all who dwelled within the boundaries of his domain—his realm—his land—his kingdom. It was *his* kingdom. It belonged to *him*. They clearly understood that citizens were "subjects" of the king. As such they were "subject" to the king's authority and "subjects" were expected to serve the king.

Representative government had no place in the mind of the king. Laws of the land were created not by a body of the citizens but by the king. When the king sent forth his word, either by written proclamation, or by a personal representative who spoke his word, he expected obedience. Whether his words were spoken by a representative or written on parchment, the hearers knew the words came with the same authority as if the voice of the king had spoken to them face to face. Whether his subjects came under his rule by conquest or by voluntarily entering his domain, Kings were to be obeyed! They accepted the king was their lord. He was their master.

All of this was clearly in the minds of the people when Jesus invited them to enter the Kingdom of God. They were intimately aware of what it meant to live under a king. They knew that a King was "Lord" and "Master" of all citizens of the kingdom. When Jesus laid out the style of life expected of those who submitted themselves as subjects of the King of the Kingdom of God, the masses turned away. Many of His followers also turned away. Some found the expectations too high. Others seem not to have understood some of his cryptic language (John 6:60-66).

Certainly, few who are on the roles of

membership of the modern church fail to refer to Jesus as the Christ. Talk is cheap. We may *call* Him Christ while refusing to bow before Him as our king. We may *call* Him Lord while refusing to submit to His Lordship. Indeed, during the days of His flesh Jesus asked on at least one occasion, "Why do you call Me, Lord, Lord, and do not (practice) what I tell you (Luke 6:46)?" In essence, He was saying, "You waste your breath by calling me Lord when you don't obey me. Your behavior belies your words. You are still subject (obediently under the rule) to the Evil One. You are *his* subject, not mine. *He* is your lord; not I."

Those who obey Satan and blindly expect a reward of eternal Heavenly bliss seem never to have listened to Jesus when He said, "Not every one that saith unto me, Lord, Lord, shall enter into the kingdom of heaven; but *he that doeth the will of my Father* which is in heaven. Many will say to me in that day, Lord, Lord, have we not prophesied in thy name? and in thy name have cast out devils? and in thy name done many wonderful works? And then will I profess unto them, *I never knew you: depart from me, ye that work iniquity*" (Matt. 7:21-23). (Emphases mine)

What iniquity (sin, evil)?

Theft! Robbery! Rape! Murder! Greed! Selfishness! Gossip! And hundreds of lesser misdeeds that diminish the quality of life for one's self and/or for one's neighbor!

Professors of Christianity Pack Our Prisons

Look who's packing the prisons across America. I spoke earlier of a pivotal moment in my life when the remnant of a man in jail for drunkenness passed out at my feet. Another pivotal moment in my thinking occurred many years later during follow-up research to a doctoral dissertation. I had performed a ground-breaking study of the development of perceptions of the personality of God among the general population[93] and was replicating the study among prisoners in the Tennessee State Prison system. I discovered that of the men who enter Brushy Mountain (Tennessee's Maximum Security Prison), more than 95% profess themselves to be Christians. What? Something's wrong! Either there's something wrong with those men's perception of Christianity, or perhaps there's something wrong with my research instrument. I reviewed it again and recalled that the research instrument had tested positively. It had been examined by a professional statistician at the University of Tennessee. My Graduate Committee at Oxford Graduate School had scrutinized my research quite closely, and had even given me an award for the research. Still disbelieving the evidence, I called the prison chaplain and expressed my dismay.

"Bill, there's nothing wrong with your research.

93 William G. Justice, *A Comparative Study of the Language People Use to Describe the Personalities of God and Their Earthly Parents*, a dissertation submitted in partial fulfillment of the requirements for the degree of Doctor of Philosophy, Oxford Graduate School, Dayton, TN, 1984. Dissertation LD00963, University Microfilms International, 300 N. Zeeb Road, Ann Arbor, MI 48106.

I've known for several years that about 95% of the men who come here claim to be Christians when we process them in." These are our state's most violent criminals. Our most hardened, most dangerous, most violent murderers and rapists believe themselves to be Christians! He did not tell me that the figures are similar all over the United States!

After I learned that approximately 95% of all inmates confined in Tennessee's maximum security prison profess to be Christian at the time of entry, I looked further. A recent survey in Massachusetts found every prison inmate to be "religious." In Joliet Prison, Catholic inmates numbered 2,888, Baptists numbered 1,020, Methodists included 617, and 100% of all others considered themselves to be "religious." Notorious Sing-Sing confined 1,553 prisoners. Of them, 855 were Catholics, 518 were Protestants, 117 were Jews, and only 8 were non-religious. During a recent 10 year period, at Sing-Sing, of those executed for murder 65% were Catholic, 26% were Protestants, Jews 6% and less than 1/3 of 1% were "non-religious."

We have been taught that *Christians are expected to live by a higher moral/ethical code than non-Christians.* We are expected to live by the love code of Jesus. Something's wrong! A recent study found that the state of Michigan had 82,000 Baptists and 110,000 Jews. However, 22 times more Baptists are confined in Michigan prisons than Jews, and 18 times more Methodists in Michigan prisons than Jews!

Something's wrong when approximately 97% of all the inmates confined in prisons in the United States claim to be Christians on the day they arrive in prison.

Are they lying? Or are they deceived?

Do they believe they are "born again" (from above); "saved" without trusting (faith in) the Savior; without having surrendered to the rule of the Christ; of the King? Early in the twenty-first century, Berna Research tells us that one third of all people in the U.S. claim to be "born again" Christians.

Has the church contributed to the delusion that Christian Faith is dis-associated from obedience to its Christ? Has the church contributed to the belief that Christian faith is simply the belief that a series of events described in the Gospels actually happened? Has the modern church contributed to the damnation of its members by giving false assurance to its members who live in open rebellion against King Jesus? Or have we contributed to the belief that "believing in Jesus" is simply a mental assent to the belief that He lived as a real person in history and/or the belief in the fact that He died on a cross? Many have been deluded into believing that the academic belief in the historical reality of certain events in Jesus' life amounts to "saving faith." Is mental belief in a series of events in Jesus' life to be called, "believing in Jesus?" Is a mere belief in the truth of some facts about Jesus to be considered, "trusting Jesus as Savior?" **It**

is not—if we depend on the New Testament for a definition of "believing in" Jesus or anyone else.

Faith as a Lifestyle of Obedience

The words "believe in," "faith," "trust," and "to obey" are closely related. In the Greek language of the New Testament, from which these words are translated, they all come from two etymologically closely related words, *peitho* and *pisteuo. Peitho* means to obey. And *pisteuo* means to trust. Obedience *(peitho)* is a response to trust *(pisteuo).*

Many years ago, my children were instrumental in helping me understand this profoundly important truth. We had arrived at our vacation site on the Cumberland Plateau of East Tennessee. We had never visited there before. Lisa, our seven-year-old daughter, and David, our four-year-old son jumped out of the car and began running toward the wooded area behind the cabin. I called for them to wait for me. I assured my wife that I would help unload the car after I surveyed the area for possible hazards to the children. I had heard of the magnificent gorges that had been carved in the sandstone, creating sheer drop-offs of more than a hundred feet. I imagined a ravine beyond the edge of the woods behind the cabin.

With a gleeful youngster pulling at a finger of each hand, we walked toward the woodland while I watched for broken glass and other things in the yard that could harm the children. Before we got to the edge of the woods, I spotted a thriving patch of poison ivy nestled at the foundation of the cabin.

The three of us squatted while I explained the difference between this ivy and the ivy we had growing around a tree in our yard back home. I warned them that if they touched this ivy, it would hurt them. They would not feel any discomfort immediately, but within a few hours they would be miserable. I explained that wherever their skin touched those shiny dark green leaves, little red bumps would appear that would soon turn into little blisters that would itch terribly. ("It will itch like crazy," was my "daddy talk" description.) After we had wandered over the whole yard and into the woodland behind the cabin, I opened the door and paused. I looked back to the children and called out, "We are going to be here for several days. Have fun. Play in the yard, but stay away from that patch of poison ivy near the back of the cabin."

Only later, did I realize that we had re-enacted events analogous to those in the Garden of Eden. God had given Adam and Eve the Garden of Eden as a place to enjoy their lives. They could eat freely of all the trees except one. Something about the fruit of that tree would harm them. They had understood that God wanted them neither to eat nor to touch the fruit of the tree in the midst of the garden (cf. Genesis 3:2-3).

Lisa and David had never seen poison ivy before that time. My word was their only basis for judging it harmful. They had no experience with poison ivy. They each had to make an independent decision. Each one could decide, "I will do what I want to, when I want to do it. I will trust my own judgment over my daddy's." And without any punishment by me, they would have suffered the natural consequences of their disobedience. Or independently, they each could decide, "My daddy wants what's best for me. I don't know by personal experience that I will be harmed by the pretty shiny leaves, but I'm going to do as he told me. I trust him enough to obey him. I'll trust his judgment over my own." By trusting me, they were saved from the discomfort of poison ivy's itching blisters. Even the Apostle Paul recognized that there is a sense in which we "work out our own salvation" (cf. Philippians 2:12).

They each decided to trust me enough to do as I had instructed. They *believed in me* enough to obey me.

The person who truly believes in Jesus will obey Him! Faith shows itself in obedient behavior. There is no saving faith without obedience to the Savior. Virtually every person who has professed Christianity has memorized John 3:16. "For God so loved the world that He gave His only begotten Son, that whosoever believeth in Him should not perish, but have everlasting life." The word "believe," as used here directly correlates with the word "obey."

Every evangelist who has ever walked into a pulpit has used that verse of Scripture to invite listeners to be saved. Unfortunately, many have responded believing that the words "believe in" call for a momentary academic belief that will assure them of "eternal life." They have not understood that **believing in** Him is equal to obeying Him**.** And **disobedience is equal to unbelief**. Those who would merely profess to believe without obedience object to the words of Jesus as recorded in John 3:36. "He that believeth on the Son hath eternal life; but he that *the obeyeth not* the Son shall not see life, but *the wrath of God abideth on him.*" (Italics added) The writer of Hebrews picked up on Jesus' warning when he wrote, "And to whom was God talking when he promised that they would never enter his rest? He was talking to those who did not *obey* him. So we see they were not allowed to enter and have God's rest, because they did not *believe*" (Hebrews 3:18-19). (Italics mine.)

The word faith in the Scripture repeatedly refers to a continuing activity. Saving faith is proclaimed by the Greek verb, *pisteuo* (keep on believing—keep on trusting—keep on "faithing"). Throughout his account of the Gospel, John used this ever-present tense of the word "believe." (cf. John 3:14-18, 36; 5:24; 6:35, 40, 47; 7:38; 11:25-26; 12:44, 46; and 20:31. Also Acts 10:43, 13:39; Romans 1:16, 3:22; 4:5; 9:33; 10:4, 10-11). *All* of these passages, including John 3:16 were written in the present (ongoing, ongoing, ever-present) tense. If the intent had to make the "believe in" a one-time, or non-enduring event, the New Testament writers would have used the aorist tense—the one time, non-enduring form of the verb.

Old Testament Image of God in the New Testament Era

Two thousand years into *this Post-Incarnation Era, most North Americans live with the Pre-Incarnation perception of the nature of God.* Although God came in human flesh, revealing Himself in the person of Jesus the Christ, most North Americans of the Judeo-Christian heritage yet view God as if Jesus had never lived on planet Earth. Instead of looking to the New Testament to understand the nature of God, even active, long-term worshippers in the church still tend to be frozen with the Old Testament image of God.

Even seminary trained ministers of the Gospel of Jesus Christ are inclined to hold an Old Testament view of God instead of a New Testament view. A pastor to whom I listened regularly during a period of my life preached fewer than ten percent of his sermons from the New Testament. He once preached for more than a year without delivering a message from the words of Jesus. Yet he viewed himself as a "minister of the *Gospel.*" Listeners had to strain to find any hint of "Good News'" (Gospel) in his sermons. He could have preached most of his sermons if God had never become enfleshed in the person of Jesus of Nazareth. When the clergy fails to recognize the personality of God as revealed in Jesus, it is little wonder that the masses cling to an Old Testament perception of God. With notable exceptions, the Old Testament and the New Testament present a very DIFFERENT IMAGE OF GOD!

Although the words I am about to relate, may or may not be true, they illustrate an important point. On her way home from Sunday School, a little girl was reported to have said, "Mama, I like Jesus, but I don't like that angry, ol' mean God." Even a child can see a vast difference between the image of God portrayed as understood by writers of the Old Testament as compared to the image of God revealed in the New Testament! If we are really honest, we may be inclined to agree with the little girl. God as He was understood in the Old Testament often is not presented as a very likeable Person.

Jesus Reveals God's True Nature

If we want to know what God is like, we can look at Jesus Christ, God's Son, as revealed in the New Testament. Jesus came as God in the flesh—God's fullest revelation of Himself. One who knew Him best called Him "the Word of God" (John 1:1-14). The written or spoken word is one of humankind's most effective means of communication. When God determined that the time was right to most totally reveal to us what He was *really* like, He gave us His enfleshed (incarnated) Word—Jesus—His most complete communication (revelation) of Himself to humankind.

Any image of God that is not in keeping with the person of Jesus Christ is a false image. Among the reasons God came in the flesh was to help destroy humankind's false images of Himself.[94]

---

94 Wm. G. Justice, *The Nature of God as Revealed in Jesus*, New York: iUniverse, 2005.

Jesus, the Perfect, Complete Image of God

Jesus is more than just a good man and a brilliant teacher. He is a person of pre-history, and will yet live when the last word has been written by the last historian. If God truly broke into history by taking on human flesh in the person of Jesus the Christ can we not better understand God by looking at Jesus? One of Jesus' closest and most faithful followers (disciples) said of Him, "In the beginning was the Word, and the Word was with God, and the word was God. . . . All things were made by him" (Jn. 3:1-3). Any reading of the next thirty verses of John's account of the Gospel makes clear that John was speaking of Jesus of Nazareth.

Not only did John make such a claim, Jesus made an even stronger claim for himself. He told some astonished listeners, "Before Abraham was, I am." He was claiming divinity and his listeners knew it. His listeners understood so clearly that they treated him as a blasphemer, wanting to stone Him to death (Jn. 8:56-59). The Greek verb used for "I am" is a verb of infinite past-present-future time-linear dimension. It says, "I always was, I now am, and I shall always be." Here, Jesus identified himself as eternally co-existent with His Father, Jehovah. We get this transliterated name (Jehovah) from the Hebrew name for God, "YHWH." (The Hebrews wrote no vowels.) He identified Himself with YHWH (Jehovah). Either Jesus is who He said He is, or He was a mentally ill egomaniac, or worse—the greatest charlatan in the history of the world. The conclusion is left to each individual.

Although linguistic scholars have struggled to understand the meaning of God's name, Jehovah (YHWH), the generally accepted meaning may be stated as, "I am who I have always been and who I shall always be." Jesus identified Himself with this Eternal One—the Eternal *I AM*.

By the time God spoke His enfleshed Word, Jesus Christ, into the world, the human race was still so limited in its view of God, those to whom He came were barely able to hear or see such a complete revelation. Only a small number could grasp the truth. Jesus met with a near-total resistance. Even after Jesus' death and resurrection, God is seen as continuing His revelation of Himself. For instance, if we look into the history of God's early encounter with the Jewish race, we see that He wanted them to make a major effort to lead the pagans to worship Him (Genesis 12:3). But with their limited prior knowledge (or understanding) of God, their minds—their spirit could not believe it. No! Jehovah was *their* God. The Jews alone were His chosen people—they and they alone.

The Church Fails to Teach Jesus' Law of Love

Instead of modern Christianity teaching and demonstrating to the society the form of love taught by Jesus, the modern church of North America has accepted and teaches the society's meaning of love. Although we looked at the meaning of love in an earlier chapter, this is such an important issue we need to examine the meaning of love more closely within the current context.

For more than fourteen centuries, the Jews had lived with the Ten Commandments that God had given through Moses on Mount Sinai. Then, Jesus startled his followers with the statement, "I'm giving you a new commandment:" "Love one another *as I have loved you.*" Many have called this the eleventh commandment (John 13:34). The God of Heaven and Earth, who had given the original Ten Commandments, was issuing fresh instructions—even with the strength of a commandment through the mouth of His Son, the King of Heaven and Earth. Jesus did not say this was something He would *like* for His followers to do. He did not say this was something they ought or should do. The Messiah—the Christ—the King of the Kingdom of God was issuing a royal edict to His subjects—to those who consented to his government: LOVE ONE ANOTHER.

What did Jesus mean?

We cannot know that unless we understand the meaning of the word that Jesus used for love. Love has so many different meanings and is so overly used that almost no one seems to know what it means.

On dozens of occasions, from a public platform I have asked my listeners to give me a working definition of the word "love." Most have sat in awkward silence with quizzical expressions. Those few brave souls who ventured an answer sounded similar to college sophomore philosophers. On far more occasions, in my role as a professional Marriage and Family Therapist[95] I have asked my counselees to give a good working definition of the word, "love." With few exceptions, love has been vaguely defined as some sort of warm feeling.

When I have asked couples who have come to me for pre-marital counseling what they mean when they say, "I love you," their responses generally can be described in a few representative answers similar to those given by others. "I like how she makes me feel." "I feel some kind of warm feeling for him." "I like being with her." "I care for him."

Are they wrong answers? Are they inappropriate answers? Of course not. But when the answers stop there, they are woefully incomplete. The kind of love they describe is not the kind of love that keeps a man and woman enjoying their relationship until death do they part. And it certainly is not the kind of love about which Jesus spoke when He decreed, "Love one another; as I have loved you, also love one another" (cf. John 13:34).

The American public does not understand the most important meaning of the word "love." And with some few exceptions, the church has no better understanding of the love about which Jesus spoke than the general non-Christian public. Also, as I have been listening for many years to God's spokesmen in the pulpits of the

95 Before retiring, I was dually licensed by the state of Tennessee as a Professional Counselor and as a Marriage and Family Therapist with Clinical Membership in the American Association for Marriage and Family Therapy.

churches of America, I have concluded that a large percentage of the clergy has no better understanding of love than their parishioners. Are our seminaries failing their students? Are our theological seminaries teaching their students the practical, day in and day out meaning of the word love, as Jesus repeatedly used it? Recognizing some exceptions, the "better educated" clergy seems no more knowledgeable about the meaning of love than the man in the remote mountain pulpit who failed to graduate from high school.

I recently listened to a seminary graduate pastor define Christian love as "the kind of love that God has." Of course he is accurate, but how many of his people understand "the kind of love that God has?" How then, can the people go home and do it in their homes? How can they do it in their workplace or when they see that a sick neighbor's grass needs to be cut? (I will tell you soon.) With few exceptions, the church is left with the general opinion that love is some kind of warm feeling that we are expected to generate. "Since I understand love as a warm "fuzzy" feeling, I suppose that this is what God has for the world. I guess God expects me to conjure up warm feelings of affection for people around me. But how do I do that?"

Of course, you can find exceptions, but these statements are generally true. Therefore, the church has accepted the world's definition of love as some sort of good feeling. *Instead of defining love to the world and then demonstrating love to the surrounding world, the church appears to have permitted the surrounding world to define the meaning of love to it.* The love of which Jesus spoke can never be defined by some kind of pleasant feeling. Feelings can shift as quickly as the wind. If I limit love to a good feeling, my love for my wife disappears with a bad bowl of chili.

During the late 1940s the church loudly and repeatedly proclaimed, "The family that prays together stays together." We believed it! We believed that a couple who attends public worship together is going to build a more enjoyable and lasting bond in their relationship than the flimsy bond in the relationships of others. We believed that the couple who worshipped together was being taught a higher standard of moral-ethical behavior than the rest of the world. We were being taught to love! But who was teaching the meaning of the word love as Jesus used it? Who was teaching the people of the church how to love? "Telling *what* to do" without telling "*how* to do it" often results in nothing!

Then, a few years ago some of us were startled to learn that the divorce rate was as high among couples in churches across the United States as it was among the general population. "What? That can't be correct! The church has been teaching people to love one another," we said.

Then we learned that the statement really was incorrect. The divorce rate among members of the modern American church is actually *higher* than it is among the general population. (There is a good reason for this and we will return to it later.)

Then someone intelligently asked, "Why would the divorce rate be lower in the church when the church generally holds the same definition of love as the rest of the world?" *We of the church have accepted the general definition of love as defined by the society instead of defining love to the society!* We have simply said, "Love one another," without defining the word for love that Christ used. When Jesus spoke of love His listeners understood Him. They understood the meaning of the word that Jesus used for love. When religion fails to change society, society tends to change its religion.

The New Testament definition for love is far different from that of the American culture within which millions who profess the Christian faith live out their lives. Christians serve a King (Christ) under whose law we are commanded to conduct ourselves. The Savior-King even said this commandment was second only to the commandment to love God (Matthew 22:39). If the commandment to love others is second to the commandment to love God, is it possible that He considers the failure to love others as the second most important sin! The modern church cannot afford to continue living in the sin of disobedience to Christ's law of love, whether by ignorance, neglect, or rebellious decision. If the church does not teach the meaning of love as Jesus used it, who will?

The basic problem with understanding and living by the law of love grows out of a limitation in the development of the English language. It is a problem of English speaking peoples around the world. When we English speaking people speak of love, we have only one word to use. Consequently, we say that we love our mate, we love our child, we love our parents, we love our brothers and sisters, we love our dog, we love apples, and we may even say that we love God.

But we do not mean the same thing each time we use the word. We may recognize that we mean something different when we speak of the love for a parent as compared to love for a sister. We know there's a difference between the love for our spouse and the love for our child. And we know that we are not speaking of the same thing when we speak of loving our mother and when we speak of loving an intimate friend. We know there are differences in the love we have for various people, but we may not be able to describe or define those differences. The differences are great and they are important.

Our forefathers, while in the long process of creating our language, simply did not create words to differentiate among the various forms of love. Those who forged the Greek language were either more fortunate or wiser than those who fashioned the English language. The Greeks coined several different words to use when speaking of different forms of love. When a Greek spoke of love, he could choose the word that would say precisely what he meant. When writers of the New Testament wanted to tell what Jesus had said about love, they wrote in the Greek language. However, when scholars wish to translate any document from Greek into English, they might have any of four basic Greek words before them, but only one English word to use for translating our Scriptures. Therefore, we end up with one word, "love" which holds several very different meanings.

To better understand Jesus' commandment to love one another, we need to look at the four most commonly used Greek words.

When the Greeks wished to speak of their warm, tender, affectionate love for family or friend, they could chose from various forms of the words *phileo* (from which Philadelphia, the city of brotherly love, gets its name) or *storge* which was usually reserved for the child-parent relationships.

Storge

The *storge* form of love may be described as an over-under relationship with one in authority over the other and one dependent upon the other—as a child is dependent on the parent and the parent must be in protective leadership authority over the child. Feelings of affection and endearment are common.

This is the only form of love that results in the separation of the participants. One of the greatest responsibilities we have as parents is to help our children develop their sense of independence to the level that one day they can say, "Thank you for all that you have provided through the years. I love you. Give me your blessing and rejoice with me as I go out into the world to build my life. I'll stay in touch occasionally. Bye."

Phileo

The other family-related Greek root word for love that I mentioned a few paragraphs back was the word *phileo.* This is the form of love we see in a healthy relationship between a brother and sister, between brothers, or sisters, or between intimate friends. Your mate should be your most cherished friend. This form of love also is characterized by feelings of affection.

In our culture, with only one word to speak of love, most men are afraid to tell the dearest male friend that he loves him out of fear that he will be misunderstood. He fears that he might be heard as speaking homosexually. Combat veterans who feel they have been to Hell and back together are likely to form bonds of friendship that last a lifetime. The bond of deep friendship shared between any two people is included in the form of love about which we are thinking. But even those combat veterans with feelings of affection for their friends may never say, "I love you." They fear that someone will think they speak of *eros,* an entirely different form of love.

Eros

The Greeks used forms of the word *eros* (from which we get our word "erotic") to speak of love that was possessive, or self-gratifying. It is love motivated by the hope or expectation of personal gain.

This word was used in reference to sexual desire or to the sex act. Because of the meaning of this word, it is correct to say that a couple, "made love" last night. Of course, this love also is loaded with feelings. We do not even wait until our teen years to experience these feelings. Those who assume that love is only a feeling, tend also to assume that sexual interest is the basis of a lasting relationship without commitment. "Shacking up" has gained respect under the heading of "living together" and has given rise to the term "significant other," typically used in reference to the person with whom one is cohabiting. In the U.S., during the period in which adults were unmarried, one in three has lived with someone of the opposite sex. Thirty-seven percent of them profess the Christian faith.

Neither *storge* nor *eros*, are found in texts of the New Testament.

Agapé

Note that in each of the forms of love described in the foregoing paragraphs, feelings were an important factor. When Jesus declared the Eleventh Commandment, he ordered us to love with a form of love that is virtually unrelated to any feeling. Jesus chose to command us to follow the way of life that lives out the richest, most beneficial, most profound form of love known in Heaven or on earth. He chose *agapé*. This form of love is characterized, *not by feelings, but by behavior.* For want of this form of love, one may say, "You say you love me, but you don't show it."

Various forms of the word *agapé* denote a

habitual self-giving love to one who does not necessarily merit that love. This form of love *wants and works for the other person's highest good*—even the highest good of an enemy (Matthew 5:44). This form of love seeks to give without motive to receive. It defines no conditions to be met by the other person before the love is given. It simply asks, "How can I act in the other person's behalf or best interests?" This form of love acts, not on the basis of warm feeling; It acts on the basis of a decision to act in keeping with that which we recognize to be for the other person's good.

Since the *agapé* form of love is primarily a way of treating the other person, it is often highly visible. (If, without your knowledge, I were to drop into your home as an invisible guest, what would I see that would convince me that you love your mate? What would I see during the course of a day or over a period of a week that would convince me? What would I see in your lifestyle that would tell me that you are consistently working in your mate's best interests?)

I really am saying that love in its highest form is a way of behaving—of acting—of treating that other person. Since this form of love is a verb, it requires representative action. This is how Jesus was able to issue the command to love.

He did not use a form of the word *phileo.* He was not instructing us to conjure up some kind of "warm fuzzy" feelings for others—even for our enemies. He certainly did not use a form of the word *eros.* He was not suggesting the arousal of prurient or erotic interests in others, although a homosexual group once revealed their ignorance by suggesting that Jesus was homosexual because the New Testament speaks of a "disciple whom Jesus loved" (John 21:7). The writer did not use a form of the word *eros,* he used a form of the word *agapé.* This was a disciple for whom Jesus had a special concern that called for special attention.

All of this shocks many people. Our culture has so limited the meaning of the word love that we have a hard time conceiving of a form of love without some sort of warm indefinable feeling. When I have discussed this with couples in the marriage counseling office, I have seen wide-eyed surprise on many occasions.

When love is limited to some kind of feeling, if I say, "I love you," you are left to your imagination. Or you may think, "I know how I feel when I say those words. Therefore, you must mean the same thing." If I only tell you that I love you, you don't even know if I mean it. But if you recognize that love is a way of acting (behaving) you can watch how I habitually treat you and know if I love you. Love, as revealed in the person of Jesus Christ says, "I want what is best for you. I'm working in your best interests and I want you to be working in the best interests of others also."

Something was wrong (missing) during my developmental years. I did not learn the meaning of the word "love" as Jesus used it from my pastors, my college, seminary, and graduate school professors, the radio and television preachers I heard, or from my supervisors in three and a half years of internship and residency for training to serve as a hospital chaplain. I had to learn it by linguistic studies in *books*—Greek lexicons! I am simply one example of the millions who have been failed by our Christian educational system. The world is eager and thrilled to hear the meaning of the *agapé* form of love. God is dependent on His people to change the society by changing its perception of the meaning of love. When Christ's world-wide body of believers grasp and live by the kind of love that Jesus commanded and demonstrated, not only will the North American society be changed, the whole world will be turned right side up. And many are already loving—already "*agapéing*" to turn the world right side up. Love has changed the lives of millions. Whether the love of a friend, the love of a spouse, the love of a child, the love of a stranger, or the love of God, love changes people for the better. Societies are made up of individuals. If the society of which you and I are a part is to be changed, it will be changed—turned right side up by people who love in the name of Jesus Christ and in the way that Jesus loves.

Chapter 8

Up-righting Our Upside-Down World

Jesus began His ministry by calling for repentance, and he closed out His ministry by calling His followers to carry out the ministry He had begun. He gave the Great Commission: "As you are going into all the world make disciples, teach them to do everything I have taught you, and baptize in the name of the Father, Son, and Holy Spirit. And remember, I am with you always." (cf. Matt. 28:19). He commissioned His followers to evangelize.

Even if He had not done so at that particular time, evangelization had been implied much earlier in His commandment to love as He loved. Love (*agapé*) for others is at the heart of evangelization. We evangelize, not to enlarge a particular body of Christ's church, but because we care about the quality of people's lives in time as well as in eternity. He gave His followers no task in which He was unwilling to lead and to give assistance.

One of the most profound and awesome truths of all time lies in the fact that the resurrected Christ **lives even today** within those who continue to trust Him as Lord and Master of their lives. Christ lives within ordinary people who are trusting Him! After two thousand years, His influence continues to spread as ordinary people continue to communicate the good news of His redeeming power to set free from the destructive forces that erode individuals and societies at the same time. Even if there were no hell on the other side of the grave, Jesus longed to see the world delivered from its hell on this side of the grave. The loving Jesus was as concerned about human temporal destiny as He was about human eternal destiny. If we are to carry out our assignment given by Jesus in His Great Commission, we will also concern ourselves with human temporal destiny and eternal destiny. This requires a dual emphasis: evangelism and social reform. Love, as Jesus commanded it, demands both!

Across the past two thousand years some people have denied that Jesus ever really lived. More have denied that He really resurrected from the dead. Efforts to prove Jesus' life, death, and resurrection only results in strengthening the believer's belief and strengthens the unbeliever's unbelief. However, even the most insistent doubter who knows history has to admit that some marvelous things have happened because of something peculiar in the power of the Gospel. And the Christian will continue to bear witness to God's redeeming work through Jesus Christ in their own lives and their hope of resurrecting from the dead as Christ was risen. They will continue to remind their neighbor of the Scripture that affirms:

> Now if Christ be preached that he rose from the dead, how say some among you that there is no resurrection of the dead? But if there be no resurrection of the dead, then is Christ not risen: And if Christ be not risen, then is our preaching vain, and your faith is also vain. Yea, and we are found false witnesses of God; because we have testified of God that he raised up Christ: whom he raised not up, if so be that the dead rise not. For if the dead rise not, then is not Christ raised: And if Christ be not raised, your faith is vain; ye are yet in your sins. Then they also which are fallen asleep in Christ are perished. (I Cor. 15:12-18)

Believers believe. They believe God. They believe the Bible. They believe that their faith is not in vain. Christian reformers believe even more. They believe in the cause they promote. They believe in their fellow Christians. And they believe in themselves. They are aware of their own personal experience with the Christ who refused to remain in the tomb—with the yet-living, re-creative Christ. They have observed God's transforming work in the lives of people they know. The more they become aware of the social changes—the social transformations God has brought about over the past two thousand years, their faith is strengthened and they want to do their part in making the world a better place. The efforts of a few will look outstanding. The efforts of most of us will be barely noticed, but we contribute our bit.

If you have never tossed a stone into the edge of a quiet pond and watched the ripples slowly extend to the opposite side, you missed out on one of childhood's true delights. We have been told that it is within the realm of possibility that a butterfly flitting from flower to flower in India could set into motion the stirring of winds that could result in the creation of a hurricane in the Atlantic Ocean. Little things truly can mean a lot. Even the smallest loving efforts of the littlest of the "little people" can have major value. When a little boy in Ohio began knocking on doors of neighbors in his block to collect money to help feed the starving people of Bangladesh, he would never have dreamed that his efforts would ignite a drive that resulted in millions of dollars going for his purpose. When a pastor stood up at a meeting of his peers and suggested that they should build a hospital in their city, he could have only vaguely envisioned the thousands of human hurts that would be ministered to in the years ahead. Neither could a man who helped a little boy build a rabbit trap have anticipated the life-transformation that would grow out of such tiny efforts.

All efforts to make the world a better place

need not result in large, highly visible results. Good things happen when God's people actively watch for opportunities to make a difference—to make the world just a little better place to live. One man, wanting to make a difference, simply planted a few trees that would produce seeds that would result in more trees for future generations. I watched my father plant a tree and smile as he imagined children playing beneath it long after he had died. A husband and wife squeeze in one day a month to help build houses with Habitat for Humanity. Another couple delivers "meals on wheels" to homebound, disabled elders. I was chatting last week with a woman who volunteers to help one day a week at the local Senior Citizen's Center.

Christ's commandment to love—to keep on loving as He loves continues and will continue until the end of time. Christ and this upside down society—this upside down world await the efforts of ordinary people who conspire to help turn the whole world right side up. The mere observation of conditions is not enough! Concerned with social evils, Earle Cairns has appropriately written:

> The Christian citizen will seek action in whatever way is legitimate to correct the evils by cooperation with those who are also conscious of the evil. In this way the Christian will help to turn the world, which has inverted moral values, right side up. . . The Christian seeks to preserve that which is good in society and to remove only that

> which is defective, sinful, or opposed to the general good.[96]

Cairn called for action. What action? The silly line about the cowboy who jumped on his horse and rode off in all directions describes the danger of riding off without a strategy. In the lines of a previous paragraph, I spoke of a conspiracy. A conspiracy requires a coordinated strategy—a coordinated plan of action. In the remaining pages ahead we are going to look at some possible plans of action. We will look at how others have accomplished worthy social changes. We can act. But we need to coordinate our action. I can say it no better than Tom Sine in the first chapter of his book, *The Mustard Seed Conspiracy*:

> You are invited to join a growing number of brothers and sisters all over this planet in celebrating the good news that the new age of God is literally transforming this present age. You are invited to unprecedented adventure of allowing God to use your life to change this world. . . . God has chosen to change the world through the lowly, the unassuming, and the imperceptible. Jesus said, "With what shall we compare the Kingdom of God or what parable shall we use for it? It is like a grain of mustard seed, which when sown upon the ground, is the smallest of all the seeds on earth; yet when it is sown it grows up and becomes

96 Cairns, p. 145, 1960.

> the greatest of all shrubs, and puts forth large branches, so that the birds of the air can make nests in its shade (Mark 4:30-32). That has always been God's strategy—changing the world through the conspiracy of the insignificant.[97]

You and I are among the "insignificant." We are the "little people" of the world. We are not the renowned. Before you picked up this book, you probably never saw or heard the name, William Justice of Knoxville, Tennessee. Among the multiplied millions of people who have gone before us, trusting God through our Christ our Redeemer, relatively few have gained renown. The probability is high that your life and mine was transformed by God through the influence of people the world would consider insignificant. But they became significant to you and me. Outside my home community, no one ever heard of Edward Cassidy. He was just another of the "little people"—the insignificant people of my community. But he made a difference in my life. He was largely responsible for my decision to give my life to the Lordship of Jesus Christ. He went quietly, unassumingly about the task of working to change the world one person at a time. God has always used insignificant people to carry out the grunge work of changing His world.

A little shepherd boy named David was <u>insignificant</u> until he stepped forth with a sling

97 Sine, p. 11.

and a stone and defeated an army by killing the giant, Goliath. A teen-age peasant girl from the remote Galilean town of Nazareth birthed God's own, uniquely begotten Son, Jesus. If God had chosen some other woman, the world would never have known of Mary and probably would never have heard of a village called Nazareth. Of David and Mary, after they responded to God's leadership, we know of them. But by an incredibly large, innumerable majority, the people God has used in a conspiracy to advance His Kingdom are unrenowned and forgotten. You and I may never be remembered, but we can serve as members of that great conspiracy to advance His Kingdom as we go about our business throughout our little corner of the world. However, if we join that great Christian conspiracy with its magnificent obsession to help change the world, we need to understand the plan. In large part it goes back to Christ's Eleventh Commandment of love (*agapé*) as He loves. That means as we go throughout our little part of the world, we will consistently, habitually work in the best interests of all others around us, sacrificing our time, money, talents—sacrificing ourselves for others.

When we serve others, we serve God. Jesus said, "in as much as you have done it unto the least of these, my brothers, you have done it unto me" (Matt. 25:40). I have a son and a daughter. I love them dearly. If they have a need and you help them, you have done something good for me. When my daughter's automobile stopped on her way to an examination at the University of Tennessee, and the tow-truck driver took her to the university so that she could take her examination, he did something good for me. I was most grateful to him! When we do something for others, we do something for God the Heavenly Father. As His children, we, too, must be about our Father's business.

The great Indian reformer, Mahatma Gandhi has been quoted as having said that if he were ever to meet someone who consistently lived as Christ taught that he would become a Christian. We as Christians have been told time after time that we should go and tell of the re-creative, redemptive power of the living Christ. The world wants, not only to hear words (that too often result in nothing more than sounds coming from a mouth), the world wants to see Christianity demonstrated. They want to see that Christ continues to turn people's lives right side up.

I am a woodcraftsman. If I chose to do so, I could earn a living at my wood-turning lathe. I could talk for a week to you about how to turn a wooden apple on a lathe, how to shape the stem on a disc-sander, and how to burn the bloom end on a grinding wheel, but unless you are familiar with turning, I doubt that you would be able to turn an apple on a lathe until I demonstrate it while you look over my shoulder. We certainly cannot demonstrate how God changes (recreates) human beings, but we can surely demonstrate the results of God's work in our lives.

Christianity is demonstrated through love (*agapé*) and there is no love without action. When God then is permitted to love (*agapé*) through us, our tiny little corner of the world changes for the better. The "ripple effect" set into motion by the resurrected Christ has slowly changed whole societies and "little people" like you and I when working at the same time for the same goal can help to change—to turn our society right side up.

It is unfortunate that Christianity has too often been understood as a religion interested only in saving souls for a grand, blissful, eternal tomorrow. From the time of Adam and Eve, God repeatedly has sought to create a Kingdom of people who would obediently follow Him in the creation of one, great, world-wide, united, harmonious, peaceful, loving society. He has never stopped calling each person who accepts Him as their King to serve as His cultural agents, working to improve the tiny corner of the world in which we find ourselves. We err when we try to limit the Kingdom of God to a future, eternal Heavenly dimension. The King of Heaven and of earth, from the beginning, has worked through human agents to create a dimension of His Kingdom here on earth for the duration of time. Those who refuse to accept His Kingship resourcefully degrade themselves and others and slowly destroy themselves and others.

Although often unrecognized, the Kingdom of God is the dominant theme of the Old Testament, continued to be the dominant theme of Jesus the Christ, and continues to be the dominant theme throughout the New Testament. Of course, we know that the words, "Kingdom of God," are not used in the Old Testament. But the idea of the Kingdom of God is far broader than the term. The promotion of God's rule over humankind as they lived in society is one golden thread woven throughout the fabric of Biblical history. God has always been concerned with the way humans treat one another.

God had already made a covenant with Abraham, but renewed it hundreds of years later with the people whom He had delivered from slavery in Egypt. When the descendants of Abraham arrived at Mt. Sinai, He made a fresh covenant with all the people. As long as they obediently accepted His rule over their lives, He would be their God. The people agreed to live under His rule (accepting Him as their King). Six of the Ten Commandments focused on the social dimension of their lives. The people of God bore social responsibilities. Each of those who accepted His rule in their lives was expected to influence their own little sphere of influence. The high points and the low points of the Old Testament were described in terms of social issues. During the high points, the people were treating one another well. During the low points of their history, the people were mistreating one another. During the worse of times, the powerful were taking advantage of the powerless. At times evil, destructive attitudes and behaviors were copied and repeated to the degradation and destruction of their whole culture, and at times good and loving attitudes and behaviors were copied and repeated to the glory of their whole culture.

The change agent that Christ established and loved was the church—not an organized body, but a body—a community of people dedicated to introducing others to God in the person of Jesus Christ and for the care of those less blessed then they. It was also for the cultivation and growth of those who make an initial commitment of Him as Lord, Savior, and King. This commitment is the most elementary and necessary beginning place for those who would serve as Christian change agents within their society.

Within the last century, the church has tended to one of two extremes. It has become so socially concerned that it has minimized its concern for people's relationship with God, or it has become so concerned with people's relationship with God that it has minimized social issues. Perhaps one of the most Godly tasks of the modern day church is to maintain a healthy balance between the two extremes. I reluctantly have to admit that it appears that the more organized Christ's church has become in North America, with notable exceptions, the farther it has grown from demonstrating love to the society in which it exists. Instead, too often it has focused on expansion without a concern for the redemption of its people. It has focused on itself instead of the world in which it exists. It has wasted time and energy bickering about minor interpretations of the scripture. (I recently heard a heated conflict among clergymen discussing the size of the mustard seed because the mustard seed is not really the "smallest of all seeds" as Jesus had said in one of His teachings. As I listened, I recalled a professor who told of a time when the world was caught up in moral degradation, the clergy gathered to debate how many angels could dance on the head of a pin.)

When the church fails to adequately demonstrate love among brothers and sisters and to its society, the society shrugs its shoulders and continues on its self destructive path. Self-centeredness, self-indulgence, lack of self-respect and the resultant lack of respect for others, decays, erodes, disintegrates, and kills character and ultimately kills individuals. Such attitudes and behaviors infect and kill whole societies. The wages of sin have always been and continues to be death. But, "righteousness exhaults a nation." Despite many failings of the organized church in America, it has and still contributes much to the betterment of its own people and peoples around the world.

Notable Exceptions

But Christianity is "working"—with notable exceptions! And despite my concerns for organized Christianity across the country, it is generally organized Christianity that is making it work. It is "working" because many dedicated people are still working.

In the United States today, Christians are providing excellent care for orphaned, neglected, and abused children all across the country in top quality facilities.

Christians in the United States own, operate, and financially support no fewer than thirty-two homes for unwed mothers all across the land. There the mothers-to-be receive the best medical, psychological, and spiritual care. For those who freely choose to give up their babies, they provide licensed adoption services.

Many nursing homes and assisted care facilities are fully or partially supported by Christian denominations.

In church sponsored and individually sponsored institutions, small and large, Christians are providing free health-care clinics, dental clinics, and eye clinics for those unable to pay.

All across North America, volunteer Christian men and women are standing ready and "on call" to respond to disasters. They are trained and organized by professionals. When catastrophic fires, floods, or earthquakes strike, they arrive quickly on the scene with food, supplies, and equipment paid for by their denominational funds supplied by millions of Christians who are members of thousands of churches. With denominational support, many have even responded to great human disasters in countries on the other side of the world.

Christianity may not be "working" as Christ

intended and as many others of us would like to see it work, but Christianity is working and holds the potential for greater works.

A Dream

Wonder what would happen if every person in North America who professes Christianity were to daily and habitually sacrifice their own best interests for the best interests of every person they encounter day by day? Love (*agapé*) is infectious. Wonder what would happen if every person in the *world* who professes Christianity were to daily and consistently sacrifice their own best interests for the best interests of every person they encounter day by day? Our current world can give thanks and rejoice in the marvelous contributions that Christians have made to the world over the past two thousand years. Though great they are, improvements of the past may be only the prelude to the improvements of the future. Even if only a relative few followers of Jesus commit themselves to a quiet conspiracy to love as Jesus loves, future generations will look back and give thanks that God chose not to let Jesus remain in the tomb.

If you have absolutely no interest in the possibility of making any difference in your world, you may prefer to stop reading. We are going to be looking at *how* others have gone about the process of helping to make the world a better place.

Chapter 9

Social Changers Have Created Patterns For the Future

A study of the influence of Christianity over the past 2000 years has clearly demonstrated that the religion established by Jesus of Nazareth has brought about marvelous social changes. In the words of Clifford Hill,

> A clear conclusion from the evidence is that when Christians are active in society with a full biblical expression of the faith in their lifestyle, commitment and use of social influence, the nation prospers. The opposite conclusion is also demonstratable from the evidence, that when Christians are not active in society with a full biblical expression of the faith, the nation suffers. When Christians become preoccupied with internal debate, doctrinal division, or are inwardly-looking rather than outwardly-

> looking, the mission of communicating the creative dynamic of the gospel into society is diminished or lost.[98]

We must *not* let that creative dynamic become lost! Early Christians were specialists in what modern Christians often call "Contextualized ministry." They remained alert to the needs for ministry that existed in their little corner of the world—within the context of where they lived. When they recognized a need, whether spiritual, physical, or social, they worked to minister to that human need. Although simple and logical, if the process was not a planned, step-by-step conspiracy of men, then surely it appears to have been planned and orchestrated by God. The principles seem too similar to have developed purely by chance. My experience has taught me that when "interesting" coincidences occur, I should take note. The mind and hand of God may be at work leading to something good. Let's look at the pattern that emerges upon examination.

The Formation Pattern

Christians of the past have formed new institutions and they have reformed established institutions. Both, the formers and the re-formers have left behind patterns.

If we study the past, perhaps we can learn for the future. In previous chapters we have looked at many social changes which Christians in bygone

98 Hill, p. 338.

years have brought about. The "Formers" are represented by those who established orphanages, nursing homes, hospitals, and schools. An analysis of the actions of those formers of new institutions reveal a pattern that may help modern day Christians develop strategies and actions to promote needed changes in our modern world.

- Early Christians consistently prayed for Divine leadership.
- They watched for needs within the context of their current lives. They practiced "contextualized ministry."
- They kept their eyes open for needs among the people around them.
- Their vision for change developed into a "magnificent obsession."
- They integrated their Christian faith into their actions by working to fulfill the needs.
- They spoke clearly to like-minded people of the need they recognized.
- Admitting their limitations, they enlisted the support of like-minded people and thereby formed a conspiracy for action.
- They spoke to the people around them of Christ, the Re-creator: the Redeemer.
- They were frequently moved by compassion. They could feel the suffering of their fellow human beings.

- They demonstrated love (*agapé*) by sacrificing their own time, money, and energies for the sake of others.
- Although limited in resources, they gave of what they had.

Those who followed the Formation Pattern accomplished major social changes with only the help of God and the use of their own resources. They accomplished without state or church governmental involvement.

The Reformation Pattern

Serious Christians want to know how: How can I help make a difference? After I have developed the practice of habitually loving in a way that works in the best interests of others, what can I or we do to actually change our emotionally, physically, and spiritually sick upside-down society? What can we learn from the past that will help us develop a strategy for creating a process for changing the world?

Early in my studies of the social conditions that are sickening the country that I love, it became more than obvious that changes are needed. But to point to social conditions that need to be changed and then to walk away seemed almost immoral. Something inside me says that he who points to a problem is morally obligated to offer a possible solution. But I was not intelligent and creative enough to see a solution.

As I have studied history from various

perspectives, I recognized that cultural changes are brought about by changing the values of a society; whereas social changes are brought about by changing the institutions of society. Then I reviewed changes that Christians of the past have initiated and wondered how they did it. The various social improvements did not "just happen." If we analyze how others have done it, perhaps we can learn to do it too.

As I thought through the changes about which I have written in the previous pages of this book, I began to see some things the "world changers" had in common. Perhaps by studying how others have done it, we Christians might find a pattern or blueprint that conspirators could follow for creating social improvement.

Then I learned that Clifford Hill and his associates had analyzed the method that William Wilberforce and his associates had developed for bringing about the end of slavery in Britain. Hill told the world of his group's conclusions in a book by which every Christian who wants to make a difference might profit: *The Wilberforce Connection* (see Bibliography).

Hill has described several specific measures that the Wilberforce group employed to bring about the demise of the institution of slavery in Britain. Wilberforce began with the obvious.

1. Wilberforce recognized that the task of changing Britain was too large a task for one man. He needed the help of like-minded people

dedicated to the task of eradicating slavery. That band became known as the Clapham Group.

2. He also knew that people do not change unless they are motivated and that love and fear are the two most powerful motivators for human behavior. "Wilberforce coined the phrase, 'making goodness fashionable'."[99] He was determined to demonstrate goodness in his own life and insisted that those involved in the efforts to abolish slavery must do the same. He was convinced that love (*agapé*) as Jesus had demonstrated it would be the spirit—the lifestyle that Christian cultural/ social changers must habitually demonstrate in their own lives.

3. Wilberforce emphasized moral values. "He set about changing the values of the nation by demonstrating that they were based upon false premises such as injustice, lies, and deception. He used empirical evidence to make a direct appeal to public opinion that changed the minds of the nation and eventually forced the legislature to take action."[100] Wilberforce was wise enough to see that he needed the support of the masses of the common "little people" before Parliament could be persuaded to enact the laws prohibiting slavery.

4. Wilberforce insisted that his cohorts must consistently demonstrate the highest integrity to all observers. They had to be men of honor in every dimension of their lives. No evidence of personal

---

99 Hill, p. 341.

100 Hill, p. 342.

gain could be claimed against any of those who made up his small band of co-conspirators to end the slave trade.

5. The Wilberforce's Clapham Group knew that social change is a process. It is rarely accomplished quickly and without prolonged resistance that required persistence. Despite their inner impatience, they knew from the beginning of their efforts that they must remain persistent. If they were to succeed, they could not permit themselves to be more than momentarily discouraged. To borrow a phrase from a friend of many years gone by, "They had to keep on keeping on."

6. They also saw the bigger picture. Although focused on their primary purpose, they also remained observant of the wider range of issues that were eroding their entire culture. While they were working to promote social reform that would end slavery, they also wanted to promote social change throughout their entire culture. Of course, this required his listeners to re-examine their values.

7. They built a community of the concerned. Recognizing strength in numbers, speaking with his voice and writing, Wilberforce and his small band of co-conspirators worked for years to build an ever-expanding community of like-minded Christians. All members of the growing community committed themselves to use their little bit of influence to inform and persuade their neighbors. Over the years, that which had begun

as a tiny spark within one man slowly grew into a raging fire in the hearts of thousands.

8. They worked to build relationships with people with whom they did not always agree. Even if someone supported prostitution or gambling (other blights on their society), but opposed slavery, they accepted their efforts to end slavery. They did not require all supporters and co-conspirators to be of like mind in all matters.

9. Despite the knowledge that a prophet tends to go without honor in his own home, Jesus had begun where he was—in Galilee. The Clapham Group began where they were: in their own homes. Jesus had instructed his disciples to begin spreading the Gospel in Jerusalem before venturing into Judea and Samaria and on into the whole world. Before going out into their world, the band of men around Wilberforce, the Clapham Group began with their own families. Few people have accomplished great things without family support—without their family as their cheering section. Blessed is the person who receives the encouraging support of a spouse! Even more blessed is that person who also has the encouraging support of his or her children.

10. As a group of men whose lives had been transformed by God through Jesus Christ, the Clapham Group was determined to keep God at the center of all their efforts. They were convinced that God should get the glory for anything that was accomplished. They believed that God was working in them and through them to accomplish

His purpose. Someone has said that human beings can accomplish great things unless they get bogged down by their concern for who is to get the credit. When slavery was finally abolished in Britton, the attitude of the Clapham Group was, "To God be the Glory!"

Even our strongest most capable leaders seem unaware of a pattern or patterns for social change that others have discovered and are available to us.

Lessons from History beyond Wilberforce

If we go beyond Wilberforce and examine other major social changes brought about by Christianity, we see that other initiators of social reform followed much of the pattern that Clifford Hill has found in his study of the Clapham Group. Indeed, we may suspect that Wilberforce had analyzed the efforts of prior Christian reformers and adopted their principles as the process for his plan.

As we have analyzed the process of social change, we have seen several things they have in common. These social reforms are easily represented by the ending of gladiator combat, the extreme lessening of abortion and infanticide in the Roman Empire, and the improvement of the status of women throughout lands in which Christianity has been the predominant religion. As we look at these and others, we see something of a pattern. It could hardly be called a blueprint because each issue that needs social transformation is different, but perhaps the analysis shows us some principles and actions that we can apply to our modern-day issues.

We have repeatedly observed that social change usually begins with one individual or with one small segment of a society. I sat in a stadium not long ago with more than 100,000 football fans. The home team was not doing well and all fell unusually quiet when one lone voice cried out, "We can take 'em. We can take 'em." Another voice joined and then another as a few began to chant, "We can take 'em. We can take 'em." Within a few moments many thousands were chanting the words begun by that one lone voice. One "little person" had made a difference in thousands. Christian reformers have sometimes shouted, but they have done more than simply talked.

- The social reformers of the past started where they were within the context of their own corner of the world. They, too, practiced "contextualized ministry." Since all else in the reformers' lives was based on their devotion to Christ and the world that He loved, I cannot help but wonder if modern Christian reformers must begin where they are: in the institutionalized church. Reformations have never been easy. They have always been painful.
- Christian reformers of the past

have recognized that they could not do the job alone. They shared the common experience of having been transformed by the Christ they served. They needed Divine guidance and intervention, and they needed other Christians of kindred spirits. They needed to form a conspiracy, recognizing that the power truly is in numbers. The more like-minded people they could add to their cause, the greater the potential for fulfilling the cause.

- They spoke of their convictions, and many honed the craft of writing to be able to fill their ideas with reason and passion. They believed and corroborated the fact that "the pen is mightier than the sword."
- They prayed consistently, not only for Divine guidance but for Divine intervention where resistance would block the accomplishment of their goal.
- They were convinced that their goal was not only *their* goal; they believed they worked to help God accomplish *His* goal. At least as early as the days in which God used Moses in the crossing of the Red Sea, God accomplished and has continued to accomplish some of His greatest works on earth through

willing, obedient, and dedicated men and women. (He even used a virgin girl of Nazareth to birth Himself into human flesh.)

- Although we remember her, we must remember that many of the greatest accomplishments were brought about by the efforts of people who were so unconcerned about who got the credit that history records few of their names. They maintained the attitude, "To God be the glory."
- Most of those who changed societies charged against evil with the conviction that even the "gates of hell could not prevail" against their assault.
- We have seen that some of the most significant transformations in societies have been initiated by spiritually transformed people who often spoke out despite their fear of the possible consequences. (I once smiled when I read a sign with a captioned picture of a turtle on the wall of a local elementary school: "Behold! The lowly turtle that gets nowhere until he sticks his neck out.") Reformations are never accomplished without risk.
- Social reformers have demonstrated their convictions by their own actions.

- They have confronted their fellow proponents and their opponents with the truth about the issues needing reform.
- They have sought to enliven sleeping or deadened consciences.
- They have accepted supporters who were like-minded on the issue they wanted to change, although they might not agree on other important issues.
- When they had aroused the passions of the populace, they approached the makers of law.
- When they went before the lawmakers, they were as persistent as they had been in all other steps along the way.
- When they achieved their goal, they thanked God for His assistance.

Those who followed the "Reformation Pattern" worked to reform existing institutions whereas those who followed the Formation Pattern were working to create new institutions within an existing society. Those who were working to reform established institutions found it necessary to seek the assistance of the powers of state or some other great power. Without the assistance of powers beyond themselves they would not have accomplished their reforms without violence.

Christian Reformers Can Learn from a New "Grass Roots" Movement

In preceding pages, we saw that successful reformers of the past have accepted help from those with whom they did not agree in all aspects. A powerful new movement has arisen (without a religious attachment). My statement of favor or disfavor for their cause seems inappropriate for this book. However, having read their operational handbook, *Army of None*, I am highly impressed by their methods—methods that are working!

The U.S. was involved in wars in Iraq and Afghanistan. Protestors marched in the streets, screaming anti-war slogans and carrying plackards. However, they soon realized that their protests were accomplishing little or no change. Representatives from various branches of the Armed Forces were propagandizing students even in elementary schools. Military recruiters were enticing young men and women on high school and colleger campuses with exaggerated promises of financial and educational benefits. The U.S. Military machine needed young men and women. Every serious student of history knows that truth is the first victim of every war. Recruiters were so desperate to recruite they were not always truthful with their promises.

The recruiters' desperation reminded the anti-war protestors that a nation cannot fight wars without soldiers. If the anti-war spokespersons could form a conspiracy of like minded people, they could launch a major counter recruitment campaign. They could accomplish more by one-on-one conversations, personal letters, and by distributing informational leaflets in the streets than they could accomplish by carrying placards and parading in the streets. A veteran of the war, in conversation with a young man, caused him to rethink his decision to join the army. A letter to a friend persuaded another against joining the military. Success! More had been accomplished by a conversation and a letter than had been accomplished by street demonstrations. At least, they could see the results of their efforts.

Success breeds success. By telling of their success to like minded young adults, they were able form a conspiracy. They would work one-on-one by personal conversation and by letters. When like-minded young adults learned of their success, they joined the conspiracy, and local people joined into groups and organized their efforts. They recruit to their own cause. Hear an initial approach:

> Ready to create a truly grass roots, people powered movement? Antiwar activism is changing. The familiar sights and sounds of protests are giving way to quieter, but far more resonating, one-on-one work in classrooms, career centers, and communities. Whenever you hear people decry the lack of large-scale protest in the United States, even as the latest poles show more than 60 percent of people are opposed to the current war in

> Iraq, remember that the model for effectively challenging war is taking a different shape. People from all walks of life are finding inspiration and success in working locally to educate students and mobilize against military recruitment where it happens. We can see counterrecruitment asserting itself as a viable movement. . . . We believe that a hundred thousand marching one day every six months is not as effective as one thousand people talking to students every day.

Knowing that success breeds success, they spread the good news of their accomplishments. Hear their glee in words they wrote:

> In January 2006 the National Security Advisory Group which includes former Secretary of Defense William Perry and former Secretary of State Madeline Albright, issued a report entitled, *The U.S. Military Under Strain and at Risk.* The report predicted a major recruiting crisis. . . . The fact is, at the end of 2005, the active Army fell 6,627 recruits short of its annual goal of 80,000. In addition, the Army Reserve fell 16 percent behind its recruiting target for the year, and the National Guard 20 percent of its annual goal.[101]

The workers for the Army of None had learned a lesson that many people never learn: Working harder at what won't work, won't make what won't work, work. When marching in the streets

101 Ibid, p.ix.

repeatedly had failed to achieve their goal, they turned to counter recruitment. One's goal does not have to change, but the method for achieving one's goal often has to change. The authors of the book, *Army of None* have an immediate purpose: to enlist the help of those who are willing to work to end the U.S. wars in Iraq and Afghanistan. However, their broader purpose is to outline proven methods for creating social change—for making the world a better place for humans to live.

Readers of the book can easily become so engrossed with the political-philosophical issues related to the current wars that they may lose sight of the gold in the methods they have devised to reduce military enlistments.

Their organization offers recommended content for one-on-one conversations, for discussion groups, letters, pamphlets, and they offer enough other how-to ideas to fill a whole book. Indeed, the authors could take the principles behind the methods for reducing military enlistments and create a working manual for everyone who wants to create a social change. (As a writer, I find myself frustrated by having only to recommend the reading of the book without giving a thorough review. However, the book is so packed with ideas, that I find it impossible to do the ideas justice within a few paragraphs or even a whole chapter. To translate the ideas for reducing military enlistments into general principles for creating various social changes, I would need a whole book—which I assume Allison and Solnit could write better.) Their book is limited to serving as a how- to manual for counter recruitment.

However, those who look beyond the matter of anti-war counter-recruitment can translate the book's ideas into an operational handbook that will help to fulfill their own efforts for bringing about social change. Although they consider their approach as an "art and science,"[102] their methods are simple—uncomplicated and require little money. They present their case only after having researched the issue against which they work and they train the recruits to their cause. Much of that training includes a study of rights of citizens to work as protagonists or antagonists of a cause.[103]

They also study the opponent's propaganda and public's commonly accepted beliefs to find outright untruth or misconceptions. Beyond the one-to-one conversations and a few letters that aim to gain supporters, some of their members non-violently attacked the advertising agencies that were creating the military recruiting propaganda. A few people carrying plackards in front of the advertising agency caught the attention of news-papers and television reporters. Those reporters found highly articulate and informed demonstrators. Advertisers do not want negative publicity against their own companies. (They have even made the creation of posters and

---

102 Allison & Solnit, p.69.

103 Ibid, p. 75.

placards into an art and science, having learned what works and what does not.)[104]

The Army of None organization has found that well-written with up-to-date information produce highly positive results. Flyers that are handed out on street corners are printed in languages relevant to the population of their immediate region. Flyers distributed to students have often brought invitations to Army of None members to present their case and conduct discussions in classrooms. (The book, *Army of None*, offers an outline (adaptable for use by leaders of a different cause)[105] for possible use by classroom presenters. They donate their books to classrooms and to school libraries. Teachers have also been pleased when the Army of None has even sponsored essay and poetry writer's contests in schools.

They have also learned that a centralized information center staffed by well-informed, articulate members is essential.

The methods to which I have referred in the last few pages represent only a few "drops" drawn from a big "bucket" of methods recommended by the Army of None. Although they work against their chosen cause, their methods can easily be adapted for those who would become protagonists for a worthy cause.

Now, What Do We Do?

Christian formers and other reformers of the

---

104 Ibid, p. 103ff.

105 Ibid, p. 88ff.

past have started where they were. They have looked around and seen the conditions that prevailed. They could have moaned and groaned to one another about the terrible things that were going on in the world around them. They could have sat down, wrung their hands and cried, "Why doesn't somebody do something?" Instead, they prayed for Divine guidance, put their thoughts together, took a deep breath, got off their behinds and went to work. They were confident that they were going about God's work. They prayed, they talked, they wrote, they loved, they conspired, they worked, and they accomplished. They assumed, "If God be for us, who can be against us?" God has never left His people to do His work by themselves. He is always trying to guide His people in worthy tasks and to "lend a helping hand."

In the foregoing pages we have seen what others have done to improve their world—sometimes even sparking and aiding in bloodless cultural revolutions. Then we put some of those trends, institutions, and reforms under analysis and found some common methods used in the past to bring about needed changes. They built a foundation by integrating their religion into their society. As they lived within their societies, they recognized immediate needs in the context of their own lives. For Christianity to make its greatest impact on today's world, some major reforms must begin in today's church. Virtually every major reform has begun at the "grass roots." Every major reform that has not started at the "grass roots" level quickly found support from the "grass roots."

When Christians of the past set about to make changes, few people might have dreamed of the far-reaching effects their causes would make on their society and even on their whole world. We cannot afford to minimize the value of any of our efforts. If one fetus is saved from abortion, the world has been changed. If one little boy, girl, man, or woman's life is turned away from destruction toward God, the world has been changed. If one nail is driven to build a house for the Habitat for Humanity; if one drinking driver has his/her car confiscated by the police; if one corrupt city government is exposed; if one meth lab is closed or one drug lord is placed behind bars; if one war is ended with a negotiated, enduring peace, the world has been changed. Christians live with the potential to participate in changing the world because Christ did not remain in the tomb. There are causes against which Christians are obligated to work. And there are causes for which Christians are obligated to work.

Now, how can we more fully integrate our Christian religion into our society? What can we do to contextualize our ministry to change—to improve our little corner of the world?

Bibliography

Aitken, J. T., Fuller, W. C., and Johnson, D. eds. (1984). *The Influence of Christians in Medicine*. London: Christian Medical Fellowship.

Allison, A., and Solnit, D. (2007). *Army of None*. New York: Seven Stories Press.

Butler, J. (2000). *Religion in Colonial America.* New York: Oxford, University Press.

Cairns, E. (1960). *Saints and Society,* Chicago: Moody Press.

(1973). *The Christian in Society.* Chicago: Moody Press.

Carroll, V. (2001). *Christianity on Trial.* San Francisco: Encounter Books.

Coulter, A. (2006). *Godless, the Church of Liberalism.* New York: Crown Forum.

Cousins, N. (1958). *In God We Trust.* New York: Harper & Brothers.

Debo, A. (2006). *A History of the Indians of the United States.* London: The Folio Society.

Eldridge, C. D. (*1928). Christianity's Contributions to Civilization.* Nashville: Cokesbury Press.

Ferris, R. (Ed.). (1976). *Signers of the Declaration.* Washington, D.C.: National Park Service.

Funk, R., Hoover, R.W., and the Jesus Seminar (1993*) The Five Gospels: The Search for the Authentic Words of Jesus.* New York: Macmillan Publishing Co.

Gibbon, E. (nd). *The Decline and Fall of the Roman Empire.* Philadelphia: Porter & Coates.

Graves, R. (1996). *The Greek Myths.* Vol. 1. London: the Folio Society.

Hill, C. (2004). *The Wilberforce Connection.* Oxford, UK: Monarch Books.

Hill, J. (2005). *What Has Christianity Ever Done for Us?: How it Shaped the Modern World.* Downers Grove: InterVarsity Press.

Ishaq, I. & Edwards, M. E. (Ed.). (2003). *The Life of Muhammad* (London: The Folio Society.

Justice, W. G. (2004*). Jesus' Silent Years: Exploring Facts the Gospels Do Not Tell Us.* Bloomington, IN: Authorhouse.

(2005). *Jesus the Maverick King.* Bloomington, IN: Authorhouse.

(2005). *The Nature of God as Revealed in Jesus. New York: iUniverse.*

(2008). *Damned if We Are Not Forgiven; Understanding Guilt and People Who Are Their Own Worst Enemies.* 37321-7635 USA: GlobalEdAdvance Press.

Kennedy, J. D. (2001). *What if Jesus Had Never Been Born?* Nashville: Thomas Nelson, Pub.

Kennedy, J. D. & Kennedy, W. D. (1999). *The South Was Right!* Gretna: Pelican Pub. Co.

LaHaye, T. (1987). *Faith of Our Founding Fathers.* Brentwood, TN: Wolgemuth and Wyatt Publishers, Inc.

Marshall, P., & Manual, D. (1977). *The Light and the Glory.* Old Tappan, NJ: Fleming H Revell.

Meacham, J. (2006). *American Gospel.* New York: Random House, Inc.

Marsden, G. E. (1997). *e Outrageous Idea of Christian Scholarship.* New York: Oxford University Press.

Markham, M. (1867). *History of England.* New York: D. Appleton & Company.

Mataxas, E. (2007). *Amazing Grace: William Wilberforce and the Heroic Campaign to End Slavery.* San Francisco: Harper.

Phillips, M. (2006). *Londonistan.* New York: Encounter Books.

Quinn, R (2000). *Change the World.* San Francisco: Jossey–Bass.

(2004). *Building the Bridge as You Walk It.* San Francisco: Jossey–Bass.

Schmidt, A. J. (2001). *How Christianity Changed the World.* Grant Rapids: Zondervan.

Sine, T. (1981). *The Mustard Seed Conspiracy.* Waco: Word Books.

Spicknard, P. R. & Kevin, C. M. (1994). *God's People.* Grand Rapids: Baker Books.

Walker, W. (1918). *A History of the Christian Church.* New York: Charles Scribner's Sons.

Webber, R. (1996). *The Church in the World.* Grand Rapids: Zondervan Pub. House.

Wells, H. G. (1920). *The Outline of History.* Garden City, N.Y.: Garden City Books.

Woods, T. E. (2005). *How the Catholic Church Built Western Civilization.* Washington, DC: Regnery Publishing, Inc.

Index

A

B

D

E

F

G

H

Q

R

S

T

U

V

W

Y

Z

About the Author

Wm. G. Justice, DMin, DPhil, DLitt, has authored twelve previous books and over 200 articles in his field. He has been a student of history throughout his adult years. He has taught the Bible for fifty-four years, having begun while Piloting B-29 bombers for the U.S. Air Force during the Korean War.

While serving thirty-one years as a professional bedside hospital chaplain, he earned licenses as a Professional Counselor, as a Marriage and Family Therapist (AAMFT), and taught on-campus and off-campus courses to candidates for bachelors, masters, and doctoral degrees for twelve different colleges, seminaries, and graduate schools. Although retired from hospital ministry and counseling, he continues to teach courses in Marriage Relations and A History of the Integration of Religion and Society as a Distinguished Professor of Religion and Society at Oxford Graduate School, Dayton, TN.

What If Jesus Remained in the Tomb?

ISBN 978-1-935434-02-3

GlobalEdAdvance Press
37321-7635

www.ingramcontent.com/pod-product-compliance
Lightning Source LLC
LaVergne TN
LVHW010055110826
845155LV00028B/347

* 9 7 8 1 9 3 5 4 3 4 0 2 3 *